KT-404-491

for **Preparing Care Leavers**

Henrietta Bond

NORWICH CITY COLLEGE

Stock No. 232 111

Class 362.73 BON

Cat. SSA Proc 3WL

232 111

BAAF
ADOPTION & FOSTERING

Published by
**British Association for Adoption & Fostering
(BAAF)**
Saffron House
6–10 Kirby Street
London EC1N 8TS
www.baaf.org.uk

Charity registration 275689 (England and Wales)
and SC039337 (Scotland)

© Henrietta Bond, 2008

British Library Cataloguing in Publication Data
A catalogue record for this book is available from the British Library

ISBN 978 1 905664 30 6

Project management by Shaila Shah, BAAF
Designed by Andrew Haig & Associates
Typeset by Fravashi Aga
Printed in Great Britain by T J International Ltd
Trade distribution by Turnaround Publisher Services, Unit 3,
Olympia Trading Estate, Coburg Road, London N22 6TZ

All rights reserved. Apart from any fair dealing for the purposes of
research or private study, or criticism or review, as permitted under the
Copyright, Designs and Patents Act 1988, this publication may not be
reproduced, stored in a retrieval system, or transmitted in any form or
by any means, without the prior written permission of the publishers.

The moral right of the author has been asserted in accordance with
the Copyright, Designs and Patents Act 1988.

BAAF is the leading UK-wide membership organisation for all those
concerned with adoption, fostering and child care issues.

The paper used for the text pages of this book is FSC certified.
FSC (The Forest Stewardship Council) is an international network
to promote responsible management of the world's forests.

Printed on totally chlorine-free paper.

FSC
Mixed Sources
Product group from well-managed
forests and other controlled sources
Cert no. SGS-COC-2482
www.fsc.org
© 1996 Forest Stewardship Council

Contents

This series

Ten Top Tips for Preparing Care Leavers is the fifth title in BAAF's *Ten Top Tips* series. This series tackles some fundamental issues in the area of adoption and fostering with the aim of presenting them in a quick reference format. Previous titles are *Ten Top Tips for Placing Children, Ten Top Tips for Managing Contact, Ten Top Tips for Finding Families*, and *Ten Top Tips for Placing Siblings*. Details are available on www.baaf.org.uk

The next title to be published in the series will be *Ten Top Tips on Making Introductions*.

Acknowledgements

Many people helped put together this book, including numerous young care leavers and support workers who have shared their experiences and knowledge, over the years. There are far too many to thank individually.

The following organisations contributed extensively to the creation of this book – A National Voice, Shaftesbury Young People, and Rainer. Thanks also to Luke Chapman for sharing his extensive knowledge of working with young people leaving care, and also to Paul Connolly, Transitional Worker, Children with Disabilities Team, Newcastle, whose advice on disability issues was invaluable. I am also very grateful to Caroline Porritt and Sean Kershaw for their contributions and encouragement. And as ever, I want to thank Benni-Jo Tyler, whose personal insight and caring, practical advice remains a source of inspiration to many people.

Last but not least, a big thanks to Shaila Shah and Jo Francis from BAAF Publications, who are always a pleasure to work for.

Note about the author

Henrietta Bond is a freelance journalist and media consultant specialising in children and family issues. Her interest in looked after children began when she became BAAF's press officer in 1990, and since becoming freelance in 1995 she has worked with Fostering Network, the Who Cares? Trust, NCH, Barnardo's, TalkAdoption, A National Voice and many other children and young people's organisations and local authorities. She has written for *Guardian Society, Community Care, Care and Health, Children Now* and *Young People Now*. She is the author of *Fostering a Child*, *'If you don't stick with me, who will?'*, and *Ten Top Tips for Managing Contact*, all published by BAAF.

Henrietta recently trained as a coach and runs her own organisation, Resourceful Coaching Associates. She is currently exploring ways that life coaching can be used to support and develop foster carers, young people preparing to leave care, and staff in the voluntary, public and independent care sectors.

Introduction

I remember the day my mother gave me £100 and told me to go to London and sign on with as many secretarial agencies as possible. I'd graduated from university about six months before and cluttered up the house for quite long enough, complaining that I was over-qualified for most of the jobs going in our rural area. Finally, fed up with me under her feet, my mother presented me with this quite sizeable amount of money (for that time) and helped me to pack my bags. She knew I had several friends to stay with in the big city, plus a credit card if I really got into trouble. And her parting words to me were, 'You know you can always come home if it doesn't work out'.

For me, it was an important step in my transition to living and working as a young adult. After some initial ups and downs, I found regular work and somewhere decent to live. Naturally, I felt hard done by on the days when all I could afford to eat was a burger. And living on a friend's floor wasn't the height of luxury, but compared with many young people I was incredibly fortunate. But the most fortunate thing of all was that I knew I had a home to return to if everything went pear-shaped.

When I first encountered adults who had grown up in care, one of the questions that struck me most was how on earth they had survived without that safety net to fall back on. I could not imagine how anyone survived the turmoil of late teens and early twenties without the emotional and financial support of a loving family behind them.

And even 20-something years later, the question still bothers me – how do these young people make it?

And, of course, some of them don't. The statistics for care leavers who are unemployed, homeless and in prison are frighteningly bleak. However, there are equally amazing care leavers who have university degrees, well paid jobs, and happy and secure family lives. Yet scratch the surface and many of them will tell you the price they paid for this success. How they sacrificed many of the pleasures of teenage years in order to become as strong and focused as possible. Or how the misery of living alone and trying to make ends meet on an inflexible budget nearly drove them to abandon their education. How they very nearly cracked under the strain of knowing there was no margin for error, and no second chance if they blew or miscalculated their rent money. That, indeed, it would be the very same "corporate parent" who had raised them who would be evicting them for arrears.

This book isn't about how to implement the leaving care legislation in your country. You could probably write that better than I can. What it is about, is a bringing together of young people's views.

I have dedicated previous books to my very good friend Benni-Jo Tyler – a remarkable woman who has used her own experiences in the care system to make life better for current generations of young people in similar situations. Benni-Jo has been there and got the T-shirt – and nothing I write can possibly be half as profound as her words on the subject. So I want to end this introduction with part of a recent speech Benni-Jo gave in her role as Young People's Involvement Worker at Shaftesbury Young People.

'Corporate parenting – that's still a very hip term, isn't it? I sometimes feel a bit like we all know what it means, we all know what we should be doing, but often wonder why we still need to have the same conversation about it…

'I was a very new care leaver when Frank Dobson wrote the letter to local authorities asking them to do for care leavers what they would do for their own children. I remember it well because I had visions of foreign holidays, driving lessons, home-cooked dinners, huge birthday and Christmas parties – the full works! In reality, I got very little. I was "too old" at 18, so it didn't apply to me! Very parental. I'd love to see the look on my children's faces if I told them at 18 that they were too old to need my help…

'At Shaftesbury we keep in touch, offering support, help and advice for young people up to the age of 25 – and our young people get this help and support even if they aren't in education… At Shaftesbury, we also keep in touch with the Arethusa Old Boys who are in their 70s and 80s – and we keep in touch with their children! We think of them as our oldest care leavers. Why do we do that? Because we still very much intend to be there for our "old boys" and never will we tell them that they are too old for us to care. After all, we wouldn't do that for our own children or grandchildren. One of our Arethusa Old Boys told us, "Shaftesbury made my life". It is one of my many missions to work so well with all of our young people that one day they might tell us that we made their lives too.'

This book is about just that: finding ways in which all of us who work with care leavers preparing to step into life as independent young adults can create an experience that is not just satisfactory for them, or within minimum standards, but is also something truly formative and beneficial on which they can build the rest of their lives. This is a book about how to do the extra things that will make a real and positive difference to care leavers' lives. And the advice comes not from me, but from young people themselves.

Henrietta Bond
May 2008

Note on terminology

My aim here is to provide clear and concise descriptions that will be recognisable to everyone, and at the same time acceptable to the people they describe. I have, therefore, opted for expressions in common usage, especially by young people who are living the experiences.

There is currently no convenient term which properly expresses a young person's transition from foster or residential care into life as a young adult. Therefore, a range of expressions are used in this book, sometimes for the purposes of clarity and sometime merely as a form of shorthand.

We used to talk about **"independent living"**, but increasingly it is recognised that very few of us live independently, especially when we first leave our family home. As human beings we tend to be co-dependent, and young adulthood is a period where we traditionally start to venture further and further from the family group while knowing we can return for protection, comfort and support when it's needed. Young animals aren't forced out of the nest, the burrow or the herd until they are fully formed and ready to start their own family group, so why would we expect young human beings to live independently at such a fragile and formative period of their lives?

Most young people, whether they are in their families or in the public care system, need a support mechanism which allows them to venture into adult living step by step, only moving on to the next stage when they have the confidence and knowledge to do so. This support should not automatically be cut off when they reach a particular age but should remain, though perhaps less essential, as the young person establishes their own identity in the world.

The term **"transition into early adulthood"** can be a helpful one – and is used in this book, where appropriate. However, used by itself, this term sometimes fails to convey the fact that we are referring to young people who have previously been living away from their own families. Sadly, the only term that conveys this meaning – and which is used by many organisations working with these young people and by young people themselves – is the term **"leaving care"**. However, that does not mean it is an especially good term. **"Leaving the public care system"** might be a better one, because the last thing we should be aiming for is to stop caring when young people move on from foster or residential placements.

The term **"leaving care worker"**, when used in this book, is intended to cover a range of workers whose role is to support young people in their progression towards young adult life. These may include social workers and youth workers within local authorities, voluntary sector agencies and independent agencies, and also Connexions workers, youth workers and care-experienced young adults employed and trained by agencies.

The term **"corporate parent"** is a clumsy one. While chairing a conference on the subject, Paul Ennals, Chief Executive of the National Children's Bureau, expressed this beautifully: 'For me, personally, the word "corporate" conjures up a distant head office and someone trying to screw money out of you.' However, the proliferation of discussions, conferences, publications and legislation to encourage local authorities to fulfil their role as "corporate parents" is a very good thing, and the increased use of the term has embedded a much better understanding of these responsibilities. And for that reason, I use this term.

Another term that may be less familiar to some readers is **"ex-care leaver"**. I used to find this a difficult one but have recently realised it is the expression of choice for adults who have been through the process of leaving care and coming out the other side. They may not want to spend the rest of their lives branded as "care leavers" but as people who have had this experience but now moved on from it, and the inclusion of the "ex" enables them to do so.

TIP 1

Set out to be a great corporate parent and ensure you are fully aware of what young people are entitled to

If everyone who supported or made decisions affecting care-experienced young people in those important steps towards living as a young adult constantly asked themselves, 'Would this be good enough for my own child?', we would probably have an almost perfect system for leaving care.

Being a corporate parent isn't always easy because it is a shared responsibility. As a frontline care worker, it's easy to appreciate why a young person can't make ends meet on a leaving care grant. But if you are a manager or accountant trying to balance the books, or a newly elected member trying to explain the overspend in leaving care services to your electorate, you may fail to remember how many times you bailed your own son or daughter, niece or nephew out of debt and treated your godchild or best friend's child to the little extras that make life more pleasurable.

This guide is based on the assumption that everyone working with care leavers to prepare them for adult life has the intention of doing the very best job they can. However, it is acknowledged that there are restraints on workers – and shortages of funding and time restrictions are definitely among these. But focusing on the negatives won't help to achieve the solutions. It's important to acknowledge that there is some great work already being done that doesn't always depend on an abundance of money or time. Sometimes, the attitudes and willingness of workers to think creatively or be that little bit more flexible will be the factors that make a real difference to young people's lives.

Know young people's rights – as a starting point

This book does not focus on the minimum rights of care leavers preparing for young adult life, but on what is best practice. A good parent has a duty to feed, clothe, protect, educate, etc but tends to opt for the best choices for their children rather than the cheapest or easiest. You need to be fully aware of everything care leavers are entitled to, so that you can deliver the best service.

Legislation and guidance in relation to care leavers is changing constantly. So everyone who works with young people preparing to leave care and begin adult life has a responsibility to arm themselves with the necessary knowledge and information.

● Ensure that you are totally up to date with the relevant legislation and guidance for your country. Also be aware of any proposals for change, because you may be able to cite these as leverage for getting additional services and support for young people.

- Be up to date with research on outcomes for young people leaving care and for those who have left care – use the internet to check these. Make sure you are signed up for services that summarise developments in law and practice. Organisations like Children in Scotland and the National Children's Bureau provide these. Try to put aside an hour every week for reading time. It may seem difficult to set aside this time, but it's important both for your own professional development and for meeting the needs of the young people you work with.

- Be aware of which young people particular legislation or guidance applies to, and get advice from your legal department or an organisation such as BAAF or The Fostering Network. For example, in Scotland young people who are living at home but under a care order may be entitled to support which would not available in other parts of the UK. In all four nations, young people who are accommodated rather than on a care order may not have the same entitlements as young people on care orders, but this may be dependent on circumstances.

- Be aware of the additional support available for disabled young people. Take time to familiarise yourself with the relevant legislation and seek advice and information from organisations that specialise in supporting disabled children and young people.

Leaving care legislation and changes afoot

In Scotland, the relevant legislation and reports include the following.

- The Support and Assistance of Young People Leaving Care (Scotland) Regulations 2003
- The Children (Leaving Care) Social Security Benefits (Scotland) Regulations 2004
- *No Time to Lose: A manifesto for children and young people looked after away from home*, written by Susan Elsley and published in 2006 by the Scottish Institute for Residential Child Care, cites areas for improvement in the system
- *Looked After Children and Young People: we can and must do better. Working together to build improvements in the educational outcomes of Scotland's looked after children and young people*, published by the Scottish Executive in January 2007

> *Leaving care for me was one of the hardest things in my life. The stress of leaving care was really bad. It's good to keep in contact, like with phone calls.*
>
> Young person's comments, The Debate Project, from 'No Time to Lose: A manifesto for children and young people looked after away from home' Scottish Institute for Residential Child Care, 2006

In England and Wales, the relevant legislation and reports include the following.

- Children (Leaving Care) Act 2000
- *A Better Education for Children in Care*, a report published by the Social Exclusion Unit in 2003
- *Care Matters: Time for Change*, published by the Department for Education and Skills in June 2007, outlines the government's proposed measures to improve all aspects of life for children in care. This includes measures to improve the transition to adulthood, e.g. 'extending the entitlement to the support of a personal advisor up to the age of 25 for all care leavers who are either in education or wish to return to education' and 'piloting ways to enable young people to remain with foster carers up to the age of 21'.

In Northern Ireland, the key piece of legislation is the following.

- The Children (Leaving Care) Act (Northern Ireland) 2002 places 'a new duty on Health and Social Care Trusts to assess and meet the needs of eligible 16-and 17-year olds who remain in care, or those who have left care'. It also places 'a new duty on HSC Trusts to keep in touch with young people who have left care in order to make sure that they receive the support to which they are entitled. The duty will run until the young person reaches 21, or later if he or she is still receiving help from a Trust with education or training.'

'Promoting Independence' noted that, between 1996 and 1999, around 670 young people aged between

16 and 18 became care leavers. Approximately a quarter of these young people were only 16 when they left care. By contrast, the typical age for young people leaving their family home is 22.

Taken from 'Background and Policy Objectives, Explanatory Notes to Children (Leaving Care) Act (Northern Ireland) 2002; Promoting Independence: A review of leaving and after care services' published in 2000 by the Social Services Inspectorate of the Department of Health, Social Services and Public Safety

Basic entitlements

Young people preparing to leave public care for young adult life are entitled to:

- **an assessment of needs**, which includes their right to:
  - – leave at a time that is right for them
  - – know what support they will be getting
  - – understand the options if things don't work out.

  This assessment of needs should form the basis of the Pathway Plan.
- **a Pathway Plan**, which should clearly state the help that a young person will be given in order to achieve the different milestones set out for them.

Consultation with the care leaver is pivotal to the development of the Pathway Plan. Additional support should be given to young people with communication needs or learning disabilities to help them to express their opinions. In addition, the following people should be consulted, unless there is an exceptional reason not to do so:

- parents or those with parental responsibility
- anyone caring for the young person on a daily basis
- a representative from the young person's school or college
- the personal adviser
- an independent visitor (where appointed)
- anyone else the authority considers appropriate.

The decision to undertake a Pathway Plan should be taken *before* the young person's 16th birthday. The Pathway Plan should then be completed within three months of this decision.

Additional material from existing plans – such as the care plan, transition plan or health record – may be incorporated into the Pathway Plan.

Often, Part 1 of a Pathway Plan is completed by the young person's allocated social worker and Part 2 by the personal adviser or leaving care worker.

Pathway plans cover the following areas:

- health
- education, training and employment
- identity
- family and social relationships
- emotional and behavioural development
- self-care skills and social presentation
- finance
- support
- family and environmental factors
- accommodation.

Each local authority or trust should have its own Pathway Plan which, as a worker, you will be required to complete. Information about completing Pathway Plans can be found at www.writeenough.org.uk, a website resource on effective recording of children's services.

Care leavers are also entitled to **a personal adviser**. This is likely to be the role that you will be undertaking, whether as the young person's social worker or as a specialist leaving care worker. Your duty is to ensure that the young person has a Pathway Plan and that this is being followed, reviewed and updated. You are also responsible for ensuring that the care leaver is receiving the help and support they need during the time of writing the plan as they prepare to move out of their care placement and after they have moved on to young adult life. The law is vague about how long support should be offered and is often dependent on whether young people are still in education or training. However, good practice dictates that support in some form should be available until they are about 25.

Care leavers are entitled to have **somewhere to live**, and the local authority must ensure that they have somewhere suitable to live. This should be a place where they will feel safe and which is suited to their personal needs and circumstances. As a worker, you will need to decide what you feel is "suitable" and what you will be prepared or not prepared to accept on behalf of the young people you work with. Some authorities consider it suitable to place care leavers in hostels or bed and breakfast accommodation, but others feel this is not appropriate for young people living alone for the first time.

Care leavers are entitled to receive **financial support**. In all four nations, young people who are or have been in public care are entitled to financial support from their local authority until they are 18. This should cover things such as accommodation, food, clothing, travel and hobbies. At 18, unless they are still in education, young people must, in most circumstances, claim benefits. Eligibility according to how long a young person has been in public care, and the dates and circumstances of this, may vary between the four nations. The Shelter website (http://england.shelter.org.uk) provides up-to-date information about support for care leavers.

Local authorities and trusts can also provide additional financial support beyond the age of 18, for example, leaving care grants towards the cost of furniture and costs associated with training or the workplace. Local authorities and trusts must provide help with accommodation during vacations for young people who are in full-time education.

Young people preparing to leave public care have **other entitlements**, including the right to:

- be aware of their rights and be fully informed of services available
- be involved in all major decisions about their future
- make a complaint, even after leaving care, and receive support from an advocate
- have access to their files
- maintain important relationships in their lives.

Remember that these things are only the basics

If you are happy simply to deliver the basic services, as required by law, to a young person in care, you are probably in the wrong job. The support, encouragement and sense of commitment you can offer a young person making one of the most difficult and important transitions in their life, can make a real difference to their future. And not just their future – but that of any partners, children, grandchildren, etc. they may have. Your determination to ensure that the young people you work with have the best possible services from their local authority or trust – and from every other possible source of support – may be the determining factor as to whether they have a career, a family and a future, or end up homeless, in prison, or living in poverty and debt. It's a terrible responsibility but also a wonderful challenge – and a real chance to make a significant difference to someone's life.

Sometimes it's only the small things you do which make the really big differences. Giving up a couple of hours to help a young person paint their new flat or ensure they have properly understood how to read their electricity bill – or simply being available to talk when they have a problem – can mean a great deal to a young person who has spent much of their lives feeling disempowered or overlooked.

Young people who are asylum seekers

Figures published by the Department for Children, Schools and Families (DCSF) show that there are approximately 3,000 unaccompanied asylum-seeking children looked after by local authorities at any one time. These are 3,000 children growing up in foster placements, residential units or, in some cases, placements with older siblings or more distant relatives. They face a very uncertain future.

There are frequent changes in the law regarding the legal position of young people in this situation and it's best to get as much legal advice and support as possible for them – and to start as early as possible. It's also important that foster carers and other workers recognise that they are not helping young asylum seekers if they cocoon them too much against the realities of what may happen, i.e. that they may be deported. It is best to help young people develop a range of strategies for the future rather than simply focus on the one they think most likely to happen.

I've been living with Sylvia and John for about three-and-a-half years. I've been through a lot in my life. I come from Macedonia and lost my family in the war – but living with John and Sylvia makes me feel at home. They are always there for me when I need them. I don't feel left out, because they take good care of us – like one of their own. The word "foster" to me is just a word. We are a family. We all look after each other. This lovely couple are the best English people I have ever met. They are always there to talk to.

Arber, 18, nominating his foster carers, Sylvia and John Denning, for the Believe in Me Awards 2005, organised by The Who Cares? Trust. At the time, the young man's future in England was very uncertain and he feared that he might be deported in the near future.

Advocates and complaints

The young people you work with are entitled to make complaints about the services they use – including the services you provide. They are also entitled to help from an independent advocate who can enable them to put their views across when they dispute decisions that are being made about them.

It is probably a good idea to give young people information about your authority's complaints procedures and advocacy services right at the start – as part of a pack of general information. Don't hide it at the back but point it out to them in an honest and open way and explain how they work and what they can do if they are unhappy about the service they are receiving.

Again and again we hear from young people that they don't know about advocacy services. Then when we tell them about a national service, the staff get annoyed with us and say they should be using the advocacy services commissioned by the local authority.

Ex-care leaver, working with young people in care

TIP 2

Recognise the individuality of each young person

One of the gripes frequently heard from young people living in public care is that they are surrounded by bureaucracy. So many aspects of their lives are discussed in meetings, written down on forms and reviewed by people they barely know, that they often end up feeling like a small cog in a very large machine. Even basic things like going on a school trip to another country or staying the weekend with friends can involve so much red tape that young people may begin to question whether it's worth the effort – or, indeed, whether they are worth the effort that other people have to make.

Feeling like a small powerless cog isn't good for anyone, so the more that can be done to develop a young person's sense of individuality and identity, the more chance they have of developing their individual goals and creating the means to achieve these.

This chapter looks at how you can encourage young people's sense of self-worth by treating each one as an individual and respecting what is important to them.

Encourage self-esteem

When I first met Trish I was stroppy and depressed. I was very low in confidence, in loads of debt, and my only income was Jobseeker's Allowance. I would sit in my flat all day with my life slowly going nowhere. Trish actually helped. She became someone I could talk to and someone I could trust. She soon became my best friend.

Gradually, Trish started to take me out, all the time making me believe in myself and that life outside my little flat wasn't so bad. I think Trish has got a real passion for what she does; I didn't ever think that anyone could care so much about my life and where I was heading. She is always there when I need her, I can phone her anytime.

My confidence has returned, I am not in debt anymore. And I have a job which I love. I'm in this position simply because someone liked me for who I am. Someone made me believe in myself and didn't give up on me when I had a strop.

Young person, nominating her leaving care worker for the Believe in Me Awards 2007

From the start of your relationship with a young person, it is important to provide support which is best suited to the individual – what works with one young person might not work with another. Some care-experienced young people have very low self-esteem and doubt their own ability to do things. Others may appear more helpless than they really are and may tend to encourage people to do things for them in order to prove that they are cared for and valued. For some, who have learned to be self-reliant at an early age, it may be very hard to admit when they find something difficult.

- Because a young person is confident in a particular area of their lives, don't assume they will be confident in all areas.
- Be prepared to see beneath the bravado and find ways to offer support that young people will be able to accept without feeling they're losing face.
- Encourage independence but don't expect a young person to enter the deep end before they're comfortable in the shallow end. Pushing them to do major things alone before they are ready may seriously dent their confidence.
- View the process of preparation for young adult life as a series of layers – recognising that young people may be more or less capable in some layers and may be ready or not ready to move to the next layer.
- When approaching new layers, ask the young person what they feel will be their strengths and where they feel they will need support.
- Never assume a young person knows how good they are at something.
- Be careful when you tease a young person. They may not realise the irony that lies behind what you're saying, especially if you're using extremes to try and make a positive point, for example, 'Well, we could ask Alan but, I mean, what does he know about computers…? He's only designed our website and set up the new forum which everyone in this room knows about.' They may take words at face value, only focusing on the negative aspects. Hold back on using irony with young people until you're sure how they'll respond to it.
- Offer encouragement and praise, and reiterate your confidence that the young person has the resources to succeed. This works well with young people. However, you also need to recognise that some care leavers who have received very little positive feedback in

their lives may not be able to cope with too much praise and may start to act negatively to create reactions and situations that they're more familiar with. It is sometimes important to wait until a young person is ready to receive praise – or, in extreme cases, check with them whether they are happy to hear it.

Make sure that you do not inadvertently patronise the young person. Sometimes a bit of humour can help in these situations, for example, by saying, 'I know you know you're always brilliant but, honestly, this time I thought you exceeded yourself'.

> *This young woman asked me to read her short story. I thought she was amazingly talented and had great potential. I thought I'd made this clear to her and so I felt OK starting to make suggestions about how she could do things even better. Later on, I found out that I'd really squashed her confidence – I should have spent more time boosting her confidence before moving on to the constructive criticism. Young people's egos are very fragile things.*
>
> Worker with young people

Try to start preparation work for adult life when it's right for the individual

The age at which different local authorities start preparation for young adult living varies. Some authorities will start work on Pathway Plans when young people are 14; others wait until young people are approaching their 16th birthday.

Also, the approach to this process varies from authority to authority. Some will have specific leaving care/independent living teams or will contract work to external organisations such as Barnardo's, NCH, Shaftesbury Young People, etc. The role of personal adviser may be an intrinsic part of this role or may be allocated to certain members of the leaving care team. Some authorities expect the young person's social worker to undertake some of this work, with the role of personal adviser provided by a service such as Connexions (in England and Wales).

There are arguments about when it's best to start work with care leavers, and in an ideal world young people would begin preparation for independent living at a time that suits them best. For the sake of clarification these arguments are listed here.

Arguments for preparation when as young as 14

- Starting early allows for more detailed and progressive planning.
- Planning can focus on many aspects of the young person's development rather than focusing too much on where they will live.
- Young people have time to develop a whole raft of skills that will assist them as young adults.
- Young people have a chance to develop a relationship with their worker.
- Leaving it too late may mean a clash with the time when young people are preparing for GCSEs.

Arguments against preparation when so young

- Very few children living in their own families start preparing to leave home as young as 14.
- Young people may become anxious and start worrying about the future.
- Young people may feel forced to commit themselves to choices at too early a stage.
- Looking ahead too early may make care leavers feel singled out from their peers and distract them from the pleasures of simply being a teenager.

It's probably safest to say that there is no right time for starting preparation, and workers must use their own judgement based on the individual young person. However, if your local authority has set policies about the age that preparation for young adult living must start, be prepared to be very flexible in your approaches to individual care leavers.

Recognise individual responses to leaving care

Some young people may be excited by the idea of having a leaving care worker and may immediately want to discuss when they can start applying for their own flat. Others may be terrified that they will be forced out of their foster placements and may need reassurance about your role.

- Be prepared to offer explanations and reassurance that the term "leaving care worker" is simply a generic job title applied to workers involved in the ongoing process of preparing care leavers for young adult life.
- Avoid using the term "leaving care" if you possibly can – though that can be difficult if it's in your job title.
- Recognise that whichever terminology a worker uses, many young people will still refer to that person as "my leaving care worker".
- Encourage young people to share with you their views of what your role will be. This will help to uncover any myths, misconceptions or anxieties they may have about the future.
- Ask young people if they know about changes in the law which reflect their need to make a gradual transition from public care into adult living – and encourage them to discuss their rights in this context.
- Give concrete examples to reinforce the options available and highlight young people's ability to make choices about their future. For example, you could say, 'Some young people I work with choose to stay with their foster carers while they are studying at college. Some prefer to move into their own flats, and others are living in semi-independent units with other young people.'
- Encourage young people to see your role as similar to that of the parent who sits down with their child to help them consider their GCSE options in the light of what career they might want to pursue. This will help them see this is not something that only affects young people in public care.
- Build on work that has already been done by others, and try to work as closely as possible with foster carers, key workers, teachers and others so that the young person realises that this is a holistic process.
- Discourage young people from focusing on their housing needs at too early an age, but prevent anxiety from building up by

reassuring them that this will be a gradual and supported process.

Be flexible and prepared to go the extra distance

I think Mrs Barnett should win this award as she is one of a kind. She is always there and listens to me when I need her. She gives me good advice that helps me with the problems I have. Mrs Barnett has a heart of gold. She isn't just there for me but my friends too. She is the only person who believed in me since Year 7 when I first started high school. She never makes me feel lonely or insecure. She makes me feel special and warm inside. When I first started high school, I didn't have many friends but Mrs Barnett was there for me. She made me feel wanted and loved, which I never got at home.

Alana, 15, nominating her teacher, who became one of the 20 winners of the Believe in Me Awards 2007

One of the greatest proofs of self-worth we receive as human beings is that other people are willing to put themselves out for us. So it's important to be as flexible as possible, to demonstrate that you respect and value young people as individuals, and that you're prepared to work in ways that best suit their personality and individual needs.

Be sensitive to a young person's heritage and cultural needs

In order to treat each young person as an individual, it's important to respect their heritage and understand how it shapes them. It's very important not to jump to conclusions but to take time to find out what is important to them.

> *I think we have a good relationship, but sometimes we end up talking at cross-purposes. And often it's because of some little word which means different things to both of us, because she grew up in Jamaica and I grew up here. She'll use a word like kettle and I'll be thinking about something you put on the stove, but what she means is the thing I call a teapot.*
>
> Kinship carer

Don't assume that, because a young person is of a particular culture or religion, they observe specific customs or hold certain beliefs. Some young people in care may have experienced pressures in their birth families to conform to views or practices they find unacceptable, which led to them leaving home.

Young people who have lived with foster carers with a different religious, cultural or ethnic background from their birth families may not conform to expectations others may have about their interests or how they should behave or dress. There may be times when you need to use your skills as a worker, or seek support from other professionals, to decide whether a young person is in denial about their ethnicity and heritage, to the detriment of developing a healthy identity, or is simply choosing to assert their individuality and personal choice.

Sometimes young people can only choose to be different when they have a sufficiently strong sense of personal identity. Don't assume that the young black man choosing to play the violin or the young Asian woman aspiring to be a show jumper are rebelling against cultural norms – they probably have a secure sense of who they are and thus can dare to be a bit different from their peers.

A great deal has been written about the best ways to support the identity needs of black and minority ethnic young people, so it isn't going to be repeated here. But often the best way to support a young person who does have identity issues connected to their heritage is to find a role model they can connect with and respect. A young person may not want to attend classes in Gaelic or displays of Irish dancing, but may enjoy meeting with a professional person who embraces their Irish heritage alongside a love of computer games and ice hockey.

If you are using interpreters, try to ensure that your interpreter is acceptable to the young person. A professional interpreter should convey every word that a young person says. However, there is always a slight risk that an interpreter may disregard some words or nuances if they feel the young person is saying something which might bring shame to their culture or community, especially if it's a culture where young people are less empowered and expected to follow the wishes of their elders.

Young people with disabilities are care leavers too

I was told that because the young person is disabled I wouldn't need to do anything except turn up for the occasional review meeting. All the other work would be done by his existing workers. That didn't feel right to me, because all the other young people in our authority are entitled to support from a leaving care worker.

Leaving Care Worker from a local authority

If you are asked to take on work with a disabled young person, you may find they are already surrounded by workers and systems catering to their specific physical or learning disabilities. Specialist staff may be working to prepare the young person for the transfer between children's and adult services. Or, sadly, workers are simply making plans about how to transfer the young person from foster carers or a young people's residential unit to a placement in an adult setting – and the young person is not being prepared for or consulted about this move.

You may wonder what contribution you can make to this process, especially if your experience of working with disabled young people is limited. However, the role you are asked to undertake with a disabled young person is not so different from the role you undertake with any other care leaver preparing for young adult life. Just as you would work alongside people in a non-disabled young person's life – e.g. their social worker, teacher, foster carer, etc – to ensure that they are able to put their views across, so you can play an important role in ensuring that a disabled care leaver has the same opportunities to express their wishes and choices.

- Make sure you are aware of the statutory entitlements of young people with learning disabilities and be prepared to ensure they are getting them.
- Remember that many young people with physical disabilities do not have learning disabilities. However, they may have physical problems with communication. Never assume that a young person won't be able to communicate with you – be prepared to find out whether they do have additional communication needs.
- If a young person has communication needs or learning disabilities, take the time to establish contact with foster carers or workers and find out more about this in advance. If appropriate, do some research about the communication system they use and get advice about how to maximise the opportunities for communication between yourself and the young person.
- Video can be a good tool for communication. You might, for example, consider making a video that can be shown to the young person to introduce yourself – so they have time to acclimatise to the new person they'll be meeting. You might suggest that the young person and their workers create a video that the young person can send to you in advance of meeting you.
- Be prepared to involve people with specialist knowledge of the young person's communication needs in your meeting with the young person, but be clear about that person's role. Are they attending to act as an interpreter or are they attending to give their views about the young person's needs?
- Allow plenty of time for planning with young people with learning disabilities. Time spent helping them to express their feelings and identify important relationships can be invaluable in ensuring that their wishes are given proper consideration.

> *You have to make sure young people have the chance to achieve to the best of their potential. What I really like is breaking things down into stages. For example, a young person with a learning disability wanted to walk to school on their own. The foster carer was very good and recognised why this was important. We broke it down into small steps, starting with the young person walking the last bit of the journey alone – and gradually extending it backwards until they started out from the house. It took a year for this young person to walk to school alone but I heard recently that they had just gone into town on their own to meet a friend – which was a huge step for them.*
>
> Paul Connolly, Transitional Worker, Children with Disabilities Team, Newcastle

- Consider using person-centred materials to help establish who and what is important in the young person's life. There are some excellent free resources around that help to do this (details can be found in the *Useful organisations* section at the end of this book).
- Recognise that it is not unusual for the foster carers and key workers of disabled young people to want to protect them and shield them from risk. This may create tension between carers and young people who are seeking to assert their independence.
- Be prepared to use tools that help to identify both different perspectives – e.g. the young person's, the carers', the agency's – and also areas where young people with learning disabilities may need support to help them keep healthy or stay safe. Creating situations for everyone to talk through the balance of risks and opportunities will often help workers and carers feel safer about supporting the young person to become more independent.
- Provide opportunities for the young people and those around them to state what they feel is working well or is not working. This may

create some surprises for carers and workers, who may have made assumptions about the young person's views.

● Be aware that the shift towards individual budgets may create significant changes in the lives of people with disabilities. Individual budgets will give young people preparing for adult life greater scope to express their choices. It will also mean that disabled care leavers will know how much money they will have in the future and can gear their choices accordingly.

Gay, lesbian, bisexual and transgender young people

A young person's sexuality and gender identity is a major part of who they are. For young people who have been rejected or bullied because of their sexuality or who have very low self-esteem, it can be important to provide services that build their sense of self and provide them with positive role models.

● Create a working relationship where a young person feels able to talk about their identity – of which sexuality is a part. And aim to show that you are open-minded, accepting and non-judgemental, while maintaining awareness of what is and isn't appropriate for discussion. Some young people love to shock and may relish the opportunity to tell you a little more detail than you need to know!

● Locate local youth projects especially designed for young people who are gay, lesbian, bisexual or transgender. Find out about helplines, websites and other services that offer advice, support and befriending.

● Have information readily available, but be sensitive about offering it. If a young person is feeling uncertain or anxious about their sexuality, forcing them to confront it too directly may not be the best thing to do. Instead, create a supportive environment and have information readily available for everyone – you might want to tell the young person that this is simply the standard information pack about sexuality and relationships that you give to all care leavers.

● Some young people benefit from receiving support from workers or services specifically geared to support their sexual identity. Others prefer to be treated the same as their peers – as confirmation that their sexual orientation is something natural and unremarkable. Never assume that a young person needs support in connection with their sexual identity, but be sensitive and ready to suggest it if it seems appropriate.

- Recognise that for some young people being attracted to members of the same sex is simply a phase (as can being attracted to the opposite sex be simply a phase for a person who later defines themselves as gay or lesbian). So don't be in a hurry to pigeonhole a young person, but make it clear that you will support them whatever discoveries they make about their sexual orientation.

- Never forget that a certain proportion of the population are bisexual. While being bisexual may appear to be trendy for rock stars, many bisexual adults complain that they felt strong pressure to be one thing or the other, and sometimes felt rejected by both the gay and straight community. Ensure that young people who are, or believe themselves to be, bisexual have access to services that will be supportive of their sexual orientation.

- Don't dismiss what you don't understand. Ensure you are properly informed so that you can signpost or support young people appropriately. Do you, for example, know the difference between transgender people and transvestites? If you're not quite sure, do you know where to find out? There are some useful websites, and books available from libraries or bookshops.

- Be prepared to recognise that a small but significant proportion of the population are transgender. Studies show that transgender people often realise from an early age that they have been born into the wrong body. Trying to live in a body that feels alien to them can be very traumatic for a young person, especially if their claims are dismissed or ridiculed by people around them. It is not uncommon for transgender young people to have very low self-esteem and to attempt suicide.

- Be aware that gender reassignment is a long, expensive and painful process and is not something anyone contemplates lightly. Surgeons usually refuse to undertake any form of surgery until a person has undergone a minimum of a year of counselling and has spent time dressing and living as the gender they believe themselves to be. Being transgender can be an overwhelming experience for any young person and may eclipse the other issues in their lives.

- If a young person feels that you are accepting of their claim to be in the wrong body, then you will be better placed to help them prepare for all aspects of their future life. If you insist on asking what "James" wants to do after "he" leaves school, while "James" clearly sees "herself" as "Jasmine", you are not helping that young person to prepare for the future.

● If you find that you cannot manage your personal prejudices, for whatever reason, then it's better to admit this and find a worker for the young person who can be supportive and non-judgemental.

I met a worker who was very worried about a young person in his unit. This young man had recently "come out" and was really going over the top with his behaviour in a way that just didn't seem to suit his personality. He'd got this very stereotyped idea of gay men and seemed to be trying to emulate some of the characters he'd seen on TV – including being incredibly bitchy to everyone around him. The worker was worried that the young person was going to alienate all his friends and get badly beaten up. I suggested that the worker should get in touch with the Albert Kennedy Trust, which specialises in working with gay and lesbian young people. They do things like recruit gay and lesbian carers who provide supported lodgings and can act as role models by showing that gay men and lesbians don't have to conform to stereotypes.

Project worker for young people

TIP 3

Create the foundations of a positive and long-lasting relationship

When I was 19, Tracey started to work with me. At the time, I was taking drugs. I was also self-harming and took an overdose. When we first met I didn't know what to say because I hated social services – they were trying to run my life. Tracey was different though. She was always there when I needed her, *even if she had 15 other young people to help. I always had social workers telling me to stop taking drugs but I never listened. Because Tracey came across more as a friend, I listened.*

I also lacked confidence and Tracey brought me out of my shell. And it's not just me she's helped, it's lots of young people in the care system.

It is like I've seen the light. I stopped the drugs. Now I've got a lovely seven-month-old little girl and I'm engaged. I've also started a job as a trainee support worker for the leaving care team.

If I had never met Tracey, I could have been homeless, an addict or even dead. It's like she was my angel and she's always putting me in the right direction. Doing this for Tracey is like saying thank you for saving my life.

Lisa, 20, nominating her Support Worker, Tracey, from the Leaving Care Team in Shropshire, for the Believe in Me Awards 2005

It's a big joke among young people that some workers try too hard to "get down with the kids". Young people are excellent at spotting phoney behaviour and will quickly realise if you're trying too hard. While genuinely young, trendy youth workers may be looked up to with admiration, workers who don't have youth on their side will gain more respect by being themselves – warts and all.

Many young people appreciate the security and solidity provided by a mature worker – as long as they feel that person is truly on their side and will go the extra mile to support them.

Young people recognise respect

I feel privileged that young people want to talk to and open up to me. If you're genuinely fascinated by young people and enjoy being with them, then the respect comes naturally, and is mutual – you find yourself interacting with them as total equals.

Ruth, Project Worker

The term "respect" gets bandied around a great deal, but unless you are prepared to embody it in all aspects of your dealings with young people, it becomes a hollow notion. Real respect only comes about when you make the effort to show young people that you are genuinely interested in them as individuals.

Ensure that you behave courteously towards young people and expect them to treat you in the same way. Courtesy doesn't mean formality – but it does mean treating the young person as your equal. Sometimes a gesture like holding a door open for a young person or taking their coat and hanging it up for them can make them feel noticed and valued – especially if they have low self-confidence.

Be honest with young people and ensure that you work with them as one adult with another. If you don't like the way they behave or treat you, tell them this – in the way you would tell someone of your own age. If you find yourself using admonitory phrases such as 'I've told you this before!' or 'You really must stop turning up so late', you are slipping into a relationship where you are taking the parent/teacher role and treating the young person as a child. This will not help them in the long run to appreciate the way adults interact with one another, and can discourage them from taking responsibility for themselves.

Avoid making sweeping generalisations about young people, because this makes them feel you are treating them as part of a group rather than as an individual. Treat each young person as though their thoughts and feelings are unique. You may have heard many young people say the same things before, but don't be tempted to make generalisations like 'All young people at your age feel like that'.

In a truly adult relationship, you should feel able to challenge the young person's thinking without telling them what to do. Instead of saying things like 'No, that's never going to work', try phrases like 'I'm just wondering how that might turn out. Have you thought about what you will do if X or Y happens?'

Starting the relationship on a positive note

If you don't get on with your leaving care workers, it's awful, because you are stuck with them for ages. But it can be fantastic if you get on well. My worker was my birthing partner – we had that sort of relationship.

Caroline, ex-care leaver

The relationship you develop with a young person can be every bit as important as the work you do with them. You can be as thorough as you like, but if you don't create some rapport with a young person, then you're unlikely to achieve very much. Nobody can guarantee that any particular combination of young person and worker will succeed (and it's best to recognise this early rather than struggle on with a relationship that just isn't working), so do everything in your power to ensure your first meetings are positive experiences.

- Don't under any circumstances be late. If necessary, schedule plenty of extra time to get to that first meeting. One of the most consistent complaints from young people is that workers turn up late, and if they've had negative experiences in the past they simply won't buy into your detailed explanation that you had to deal with an emergency. They will see it as a lack of respect on your side.
- Try to find out as much as possible about the young person before the meeting – many young people in care complain that they have to tell their story to every new worker.
- Suggest some possible venues where you might meet, offering a

range of options for the young person to choose from. Don't assume every young person wants to meet in a fast-food restaurant.

- Don't turn up with a briefcase, get out your laptop or produce a file. Young people frequently complain that this makes them feel very exposed in public places.

- Treat this first meeting as a "getting to know each other session". Don't expect to achieve any work-related goals at this stage.

- Make it clear to the young person that you've taken the time to read their files but are interested in getting to know a bit more about them. Prepare some questions that will help you to do this, for example 'I've seen that you won a medal for swimming last year. Do you still swim regularly?'

- Try to find common interests that might create some mutual ground between you and the young person – e.g. music, films, sports, etc. This helps to build rapport.

- Negotiate with young people about how you will work together – don't just read them the policies.

- Ask young people to tell you what works well for them, what doesn't and what they expect of you. Young people in public care have often become experienced "consumers" of workers and have strong views about how things should be.

- Be realistic about what you can offer. Point out any constraints you might have – and be sure to explain why that is the case.

- Don't be tempted to make promises you might not be able to keep. It's much better to let your actions speak for themselves as the relationship develops.

- The best promise you can make is to tell the young person that you will be honest and open with them and keep them updated about what is happening.

Make activities more interesting and more educational – meet at a museum or a library. If you're walking round a museum and chatting with a young person, it's much more friendly. An informal visit feels much more relaxed for the young person.

Ex-care leaver working with care-experienced young people

Staying in touch

You may need to be flexible in the way you keep in touch with young people or the times you arrange to meet with them. Many young people have mobile phones rather than landlines. Texts are very popular for young people and can be an effective way to stay in touch. Don't automatically expect young people to return your calls but be prepared to ring them back. Be prepared to ring, text, ring back and email.

Can you get resources to buy phone cards for the young people you work with? This could work as an incentive to encourage them to return your calls if you explain that you are only able to continue giving them out to people who ring you back.

Some young people prefer to stay in touch via email, but don't assume all young people have regular access to the internet. They may only get to use it infrequently.

Consider creating a social networking site to stay in touch with young people (e.g. MySpace). You can restrict access only to those young people you work with.

> *When young people are under a lot of pressure they need some space for themselves and often go off the radar for a bit. They won't return your calls or texts for a while and you can get worried about them. Don't panic too soon if this happens, but gently keep up the calls and texts until you manage to get through to them.*
>
> *Maggie, Youth Worker*

When the relationship isn't working

How will you know if the relationship isn't working? Probably because you feel a lack of rapport between you and the young person – or because it seems that the young person disagrees with, or seems unappreciative of, everything you suggest. You may feel a sense of antipathy or even hostility from them. For some workers, this is an interesting challenge and they will enjoy trying to win the young person's trust. But there may be times when you feel that the young person is failing to get the best from this relationship because their feelings towards you are getting in the way of productive work together.

- Before you make any decisions, take the time to talk things through with the young person.
- Take time to talk through the situation with a supervisor.
- Don't assume the young person feels the same as you. Some young people really struggle to maintain relationships, and what you perceive as a poor relationship may, for them, be a significant improvement on previous relationships. They may be getting more out of it than you realise.
- Approach the discussion constructively. Don't be tempted to say things like, 'I don't think you like me', but instead say something like, 'I'm wondering how this is working out for you. I'd like to hear what you feel is working or not working.'
- Encourage the young person to help find the solutions. Ask open questions which encourage them to make constructive suggestions about how things could work differently.
- Be clear about your own limits. If you feel a young person is abusive or consistently disrespectful, you need to make them aware of this and explain that you are not prepared to work with that behaviour.
- Make sure you have some support for times when you feel undervalued by the young people you work with. And be prepared to seek help from your supervisor if you feel a relationship is becoming unworkable.

Avoid bringing in personal baggage

Cynical, system-weary teenagers may find it easier to connect with a worker whom they know has been in a similar position to themselves. So it's no wonder that some very effective work in preparing young people for adult living is done by young adults who are themselves care experienced.

However, a young adult – or even a more mature social worker who is care experienced – can only fulfil this role if they are able to separate their personal baggage from the experiences of the young people with whom they are working. Not everyone who is care experienced will be able to support others, and it's important that this is acknowledged.

> *Nobody understands what's inside someone else's head. So even if you've been in a similar situation, you mustn't bring this into your work.*
>
> *Care-experienced young adult, working with care-experienced young people*

- Ensure that you receive the appropriate training and support to enable you to fulfil your role in a professional way.
- It's OK to acknowledge mutual areas of understanding, e.g. 'Yes, the system can be really frustrating, can't it!', but it isn't appropriate to discuss details of your personal experiences.
- Avoid expressions like 'I know exactly what you mean', because none of us can ever fully understand how another human being feels – even if we have been through similar experiences.
- Be aware of any emotional triggers in your own life and make sure you are able to keep personal baggage under control when you are discussing issues affecting the young person.
- There are likely to be times when something a young person tells you triggers a painful personal memory. Ensure you have a supervisor, senior colleague or someone like a therapist or counsellor you can speak to when this happens.

TIP 4

Create a great Pathway Plan that truly reflects the individual young person

A Pathway Plan should be interactive and developed with the young person. It should be a living, breathing document which reflects what the young person wants. It should always be a tool rather than a straitjacket. If it's in the plan that Janet is going to train to be a plumber but then she does exceptionally well in GCSEs and now wants to go on and do "A" levels, then the plan should be able to change with the circumstances.

What's so useful about Pathway Plans is that they require local authorities to put down in black and white their commitment to actions on behalf of the young person, and who is going to do what. The other day I heard about a young woman who was crying on the bus on the way to do her "A" levels. But she wasn't crying about the stress of the exam, or because her boyfriend had split up with her or any of the usual things 17-year-olds cry about, it was because she was approaching her 18th birthday and didn't have a clue where she'd be living in a few weeks time. Pathway Plans are a good way of giving young people stability to make sure that doesn't happen.

Luke Chapman, National Co-ordinator of Care Leavers Services, Foster Care Associates

Pathway Plans are vital tools for ensuring that young people in care can sleep at night, without a nagging sense of uncertainty. Although there are requirements for Pathway Plans to be completed within a given timeframe (usually three months), try not to rush into creating the Pathway Plan until you have taken time to establish a proper working relationship with the young person. That way you can work together most effectively.

Each local authority should have its own Pathway Plan encompassing the requirements laid out in the chapter on Tip 1.

- Be creative in the way you approach the Pathway Plan. You want to keep the young person as interested and engaged as possible and you may need to use a variety of approaches to do this, depending on the individual. Although you need to end up with a clear plan on paper, the way you achieve this can be varied and creative.

- Start by helping the young person to develop awareness of, and opinions about, their situation, their rights and the opportunities open to them.
- Encourage young people to visit the websites of organisations representing young people in care, especially those that run forums where young people can exchange views about the care system and issues around preparing for young adult life.
- Encourage young people to join local groups and forums or attend events which promote participation among care-experienced young people. This is a useful way of increasing their awareness of the issues affecting their lives. They will also have opportunities to learn from other young people who are care experienced by exchanging information and anecdotes.
- It's a basic technique, but working with large sheets of paper or flipcharts and coloured markers and spreading out sheets of paper around the room usually feels much more engaging than simply sitting down with a notepad and a pen. Seeing their life writ large on paper can also give a young person a sense of self-worth – especially if you ensure they have a strong sense of ownership about the information. Even if the young person doesn't want the sheets afterwards, treat the paper with respect, folding it carefully and putting it away with your notes.
- Encourage young people to be creative in the way they express who and what is important to them. For example, cutting up magazines to create collages about themselves, their hobbies, their likes and dislikes, or to express their points of view, can be a good starting point for discussion.
- Poetry, drama, music and puppetry can be great ways for young people to pinpoint issues that are important to them, so look out for workshop opportunities they can tap into. Maybe you will be able to attend some activities with them or use discussions about the workshops to identify issues that are important to them.
- Metaphors can be an effective way of helping young people relate to abstract concepts in their lives. If they are keen on sports, they may like to think about the type of "training and preparation" they need to do to get "fit enough" for the move to their own

flat. If they were forming a band, who would they want to join them in that band or who would they take with them when they go on tour – i.e. who will be important in their lives as they move from their foster placement to college?

- Metaphors around journeys can be helpful in encouraging young people to draw the "route" they see ahead of them and think about the positive and negative things which may lay ahead and the "equipment" and companions they will need to help them cope with challenges on the way.

- Use a cinema visit, video or TV programme as the basis for discussions about the lifestyles, choices and dilemmas facing fictional characters or real people. What would they do in this person's situation? What choices would they make? What do they like or not like about this person's lifestyle, and how does this relate to their own aspirations?

Helping young people create focus for their lives

Some young people will have very clear ideas of the type of life they want, their long-term ambitions and their priorities. Others may have only the vaguest idea about what they want and find it very hard to envisage any life beyond their current circumstances. If young people are struggling to envisage their future, you might consider accessing some services that will help them to do this.

Life coaching, which is delivered to high professional standards and which totally respects the individual agenda of the young person, can be very beneficial. As a trained coach, I have seen some wonderful results from using coaching with young people who have recently left public care. Through the coaching process, young people are able to explore the different options open to them and identify issues that are important to them.

Sadly, life coaching is still an unregulated profession. However, there are several international organisations that provide codes of ethics, standards of practice and accreditation for coaches, so look out for coaches who promote their adherence to these standards of practice. Anyone thinking of using a coach to work with young people should find out about the working ethos of the coach, ask for references and a CRB check, and also ask for a free session for yourself to experience their style of working. If you feel the coach is respectful and fully focused on your agenda, but at the same time offers you insights and challenges without trying to lead you or force their views on you, then they are probably trained in a co-active approach to coaching. This method is more likely to succeed with young people, who will value the fact that the coach is focused totally on their agenda, is helping them to find their own answers and solutions, and is not simply someone who thinks they know best about young people's lives.

Coaching, however, isn't a mystic art and there are elements of coaching which workers can learn quite easily and apply with young people. *The Coaching Manual: The definitive guide to the processes, principles and skills of personal coaching*, by Julie Starr (published by Prentice Hall, 2003), is highly valued on accredited coaching courses. It is also speaks a language which will be more accessible to social workers and youth workers than some of the quick-fix business-oriented approaches to coaching that are on the market.

> *I only went to please my worker and I thought it would be a bit like a session with my key worker, but it wasn't... I was in control all the time, and the coach was dead respectful and helped me get where I wanted to... It was like I couldn't believe how much I got out of those sessions.*
>
> *Young person taking part in coaching*

Mentoring can also be a valuable tool for helping young people to create aspirations and think about possibilities open to them. The topic of mentoring is covered in the next chapter.

TIP 5

Have high aspirations for young people and encourage them to fulfil their potential

I moved to Sue and Tony's six days before Christmas, when I was nearly 16. They barely knew me but welcomed me into their home and gave me a fabulous Christmas... By January, I knew I wanted to

> *stay and they knew they wanted to look after me.*
> *The problem was that they were only respite carers*
> *and, as I was 16, I was encouraged to leave and go*
> *into supported lodgings. But they fought for me,*
> *went to panel and became my carers.*
>
> *When most people had given up on me, they saw*
> *a young person who needed love, guidance and*
> *support. They gave me all of these things – helping*
> *me to get 11 GCSEs and then A Levels against all*
> *the odds.*
>
> *Sophy, 21, nominating her foster carers for the Believe in Me*
> *Awards 2007*

In the past, many young people in care slipped through the academic net because social workers, foster carers and teachers were reluctant to put additional pressure on a young person who had already experienced so much upheaval in their life. While the intention behind this was a kind one, the result was that many capable young people failed to achieve because nobody was motivating them. They became part of those very worrying statistics which are so frequently used to demonstrate the disadvantages experienced by young people in care.

Care Leavers and educational attainment

> *Statistics from the Rainer website*
> *(www.raineronline.org), show that:*
>
> - 11% of children in care gained five good GCSEs in
>   2005, compared to 56% in all children.
> - At age 19, 19% of care leavers are in further education
>   and 6% are in higher education. This compares to
>   38% of all young people in some form of education
>   at age 19.

- Over 30% of care leavers are not in education, training or employment at age 19, compared to 13% of all young people.
- The proportion of care leavers known to be participating in education, training or employment at age 19 has increased by 8% since the Children (Leaving Care) Act 2000 came into effect. But rates haven't increased as quickly for young people as a whole.

Become as familiar as possible with educational opportunities and pass information on to young people

Become as knowledgeable as possible about current education systems and make links with colleagues in schools and in education and career services. Visit www.bbc.co.uk/radio1/onelife/education for information about current qualifications and make young people aware of this resource. Look out for really useful resources like the guide *Who Cares? About going to university: a guide for managers, practitioners and carers, supporting young people 14–21 in and leaving care, to go to university* (published by The Who Cares? Trust and Department for Education and Skills). It also covers qualifications, and some further education (FE) and higher education (HE) courses as well. There is also a companion guide for young people.

Most of the information below is adapted from the guide for managers, practitioners and carers.

- Young people choose their GCSE subjects during Year 9. Most GCSE course take two years at school but can be taken in one year at an FE college. There are over 50 subjects to choose from, although these will not be available at every school or college.
- Maths, English and a science subject at Grade C or above are needed for entry to most HE courses.
- Most GCSE subjects include coursework and there is a risk that young people will lose this as they move between placements or schools. Ensure that they are given the support and equipment to store their completed assignments in a safe place and to keep their own copies.

- If young people have disappointing GCSE results, it is important to find out what went wrong. Wherever possible, it is a good idea to encourage young people to retake these, as lack of GCSEs may hold them back later on. Returning to the familiarity of school with additional support to regain their confidence may be the best option for them, but others may feel that moving to an FE college will provide an environment where they can make a fresh start.
- There are two different types of advanced level qualifications:
    - General Certificate of Education (GCE)
    - Vocational Certificate of Education (VCE).
- There are two levels of a GCE: advanced subsidiary (A/S level) and Advanced (A level). These are the most commonly taken form of GCEs.
- VCE or vocational A levels are less common. They can be studied at three levels: advanced subsidiary (A/S), advanced (A level) or double (which allows students to mix academic and vocational subjects).
- Many young people prefer to go to college rather than take A levels at school because they prefer to be in a more flexible, adult environment. However, some struggle with the freedom that college allows and might find it easier to focus on tasks and deadlines in the school environment with which they have become familiar. So ensure that young people are aware of the different routes and options available to them and have a chance to weigh up the advantages and disadvantages.
- Honours degrees usually take three to four years of full-time study, although some students may be able to study part time. Students are assessed through coursework, exams and a final dissertation. Without the dissertation, a student can be awarded a general degree rather than an honours degree.
- Some students may be better suited to a Foundation Degree, which is offered by universities, FE and HE colleges. This is available full time over two years or part time over three to four years. Students can progress to further professional qualifications or a degree by undertaking a further 12 to 15 months of study.
- Some students may want to continue their education through a further degree such as a Masters. This may improve their career prospects but they also need to be aware that the age at which they start further degrees may affect the funding they receive from

their local authority.

- In certain circumstances, young people may be able to study part time or through distance learning courses such as those offered by the Open University. This can enable them to work while studying but may also make it harder for them to focus on their course work. They may also miss out on the social and supportive aspects of university or college life, so the advantages and disadvantages for the individual need to be carefully weighed up.

- Some young people may have qualifications obtained while living or studying in another country, and it's important to find out whether their qualifications are recognised in the UK. The British Council website lists all examination bodies in the UK (www.britishcouncil.org) and the European Gateway to Recognition of Academic and Professional Qualifications also provides useful information (www.enic-naric.net).

- Some young people may be best suited to a work-related course such as an HNC (Higher National Certificate) or HND (Higher National Diploma). These are work-related courses provided by HE and FE colleges. An HNC takes a year full time and two years part time. An HND takes two years full time, and can also be taken part time. There are courses in a very wide range of subjects, and entry requirements are lower than for a degree. After completing an HNC or HND, a young person may be eligible to join a related degree course in the second or third year.

- NVQs and BTECs are based on an individual's ability to gain and demonstrate vocational skills:
    - There are five levels of NVQs.
    - There are three levels of BTEC qualifications: National Award, National Certificate and National Diploma.
  NVQs and BTECs are valued by many companies who recognise the need for staff to have practical preparation and training for the post, and for some jobs NVQs are essential. However, some universities and employers do not recognise the value of NVQs and BTECs, so make sure this issue has been considered before a young person chooses this option.

- Modern apprenticeships combine work and study. They lead to NVQs, a Key Skills qualification and, in most cases, a technical certificate such as a BTEC or City and Guilds qualification.

- Access courses prepare mature students for entry into higher education by furnishing them with the skills and knowledge required for a diploma or university course. Access courses can be particularly beneficial for young people who want to progress to higher education after a disrupted schooling experience.

- There are national and local schemes that support young people who are struggling or disengaged from education – for example, those run by Rainer, Barnardo's and NCH.
- Find out about financial support that may be available for studying; a useful starting point is www.lifelonglearning.co.uk.moneytolearn.
- Become familiar with support for disabled students. *Bridging the Gap*, for example, is a guide to the allowances for disabled students in higher education, at www.studentfinancedirect.co.uk.
- Encourage young people to achieve educationally. But don't expect all young people to choose the academic route, and don't regard them in any way as opting for second best if they choose a more vocational route.
- Ensure that resources will be available to support young people undertaking education and training, and be aware of all the grants they might be eligible for.

I came across this case of a young man who needed particular boots for his training – they were quite expensive and the young person, who'd been in care, just couldn't afford them. I don't know what happened in the end but I sincerely hope he wasn't forced to give up the course because he couldn't afford this essential piece of equipment.

Voluntary sector trainer

Don't be afraid to push young people

The success of events such as the Believe in Me Awards 2005 and 2007, organised by The Who Cares? Trust in partnership with organisations such as SCIE (Social Care Institute for Excellence) and the DfES, highlight how much young people themselves believe they can achieve when other people have faith in them – and demonstrate that faith. For the Believe in Me Awards, young people from England, Scotland and Wales were offered the opportunity to nominate adults who had made a significant difference to their lives. The winning nominations were split fairly equally between foster carers, teachers, residential workers and leaving care workers. In their nominations, many young people cited the adult's belief in them and encouragement in areas of their lives such as education, hobbies, support with emotional issues and relationships, and a general sense of the adult wanting and expecting the very best for them – and not being afraid to push them a bit when they were ready to give up.

As a worker you can:

- Have high aspirations for all the young people you work with and clearly demonstrate that you believe in their potential. Don't be prepared to settle for anything for a young person which you wouldn't be happy to accept for a child of your own.
- Encourage young people to get the best out of their education by helping them recognise what they can achieve. Provide support and encouragement and always ensure that you acknowledge effort and progress.
- Make it clear to young people that you value effort as much as outcomes. So don't fail to push young people for whom academic work comes easily – if they're not encouraged to maintain efforts and stretch themselves they may slip into a pattern of getting by with minimum effort.
- Encourage others to motivate young people to do their best at school. Carers or teachers may be reluctant to push a young person who they feel is having a very difficult time. But without motivation – and of course the accompanying praise for making the effort – many capable young people will not achieve their potential.
- Make sure you have a fully rounded picture of the young person – their aspirations, hobbies and personal motivations – and the skills and abilities they possess, as well as their academic potential.
- Work closely with schools, foster carers, Connexions and other careers advisory services to ensure that they also have a full picture of the young person. They may be discounting the skills and resilience a young person has shown in very difficult circumstances because they are not aware of this. You may need to work

supportively with the young person to gain their permission to share some of this information with teachers or tutors.

- Find out abut the opportunities young people have for doing homework and researching information on the internet. A young person living with foster carers or in a residential unit may be struggling to gain access to a computer that is shared by many members of the household. This may have a significant impact on their ability to complete homework or assignments. They may also struggle to find somewhere quiet to study.

- Develop a knowledge of local homework clubs, Saturday clubs, centres offering free internet access, libraries and other places where young people can go to study and receive support with their work.

- Be prepared to challenge an opinion that a young person can't do something that means a lot to them. Instead, try to work with schools or careers advisers and foster carers to see if compromises can be found. For example, the young person may not be ready yet for the responsibilities and pressures of university, but they may be able to do a foundation course to prepare them.

- Don't overlook the major role foster carers often play in fighting for young people's rights to get the best from education. They can be great allies, so be prepared to listen to their point of view and try to establish positive relationships as early as possible.

- Be aware of the situations and current legislation surrounding young people and part-time education and how this may impact on their benefits. Work creatively with colleagues to try and find compromises.

- Create opportunities to celebrate young people's success – in whatever format that takes. Families often motivate and reward their children for particular achievements – can you do the same? Or can you ensure that foster carers are in a position to do this? Maybe you can persuade a local cinema to donate some free tickets on a regular basis which can be given out to young people who have made the most significant progress in recent months.

- Remember that certificates are valuable to young people who are trying to build up a portfolio to demonstrate their skills to colleges or employers. Don't forget to produce these if you are organising relevant events, and also encourage others who are organising events to provide them.

Be realistic about young people's potential

This may seem contradictory to the section above but there is a difference between motivating and supporting a young person, and encouraging them to set themselves impossible goals which will dishearten them and create a sense of failure. Helping a young person to break down their ambitions into more manageable steps may be the best way to help a young person achieve their ultimate goal.

> *I was working with a young person who really wanted to be a chef. However, when he realised how much studying was involved, he started to panic and I was worried he might drop out altogether. I've helped him find a part-time catering course where he can return to study more gently, and this seems to be working well for him.*
>
> Care Leavers Support Worker

Promote spare-time activities for young people in care

> *A young woman growing up in foster care was helped to keep up her interest in learning the flute by her foster carers, her school and her social worker over ten years. As she became a better musician, she needed more expensive instruments but the adults involved ensured that she secured them. Today, this young woman is a university graduate and working as a qualified music teacher...*
>
> *For another less academically able or motivated young woman, participation in her beloved school choir served as an important incentive for her to remain in school beyond school leaving age. The choir may not have helped her achieve better results*

> *but delaying exit from school may have assisted her to develop important social skills and assets...*
>
> *Taken from 'Spare time activities for young people in care: what can they contribute to educational progress', by Robbie Gilligan, Adoption & Fostering, p. 97, 32:1, 2007*

In the above article, Gilligan cites a number of studies from the USA and New Zealand which suggest there is a link between young people taking part in extracurricular activities and educational achievements. While there has not been a great deal of research into the specific experiences of care-experienced young people, an Irish study (F Daly and R Gilligan, *Lives in Foster Care: The educational and social support experiences of young people aged 13–14 in long-term foster care*, 2005) found a statistically significant connection between a young person receiving 'social support from friendships and participating in hobbies/activities' and 'positive educational and schooling experiences' (quoted in the Gilligan article, p. 94).

Gilligan is cautious about claiming that extracurricular activities by themselves are likely to increase young people's academic achievements, but he recognises that there are a number of factors that may be beneficial. According to Gilligan, extracurricular activities can increase a young person's motivation to engage with education and school activities, and 'spare time activities are one of the means open to carers and other concerned adults in terms of influencing the educational progress and motivation of young people in care'.

To encourage young people to develop through extracurricular activities, you can:

- Take time to find out what "lights up" the young person. They may not readily identify a specific hobby but you will often discover that they have interests and issues they care deeply about.
- Check out whether young people have been able to pursue hobbies which were important to them in the past. Is there something they have stopped doing because nobody realised it was significant to them, or because it was too difficult or too

expensive to pursue? Are there ways the young person could be reintroduced to this activity or is there a new but related activity they might like to try out?

> *Riding lessons aren't cheap but often local stables are keen to recruit some weekend or holiday helpers. Young people get the experience of working with horses, meet people and make friends with others who share their interests – and in return get some free riding lessons.*
>
> Worker with young people

- Use your meetings with young people as opportunities to create new interests – for example, suggest meeting at a museum or art gallery.
- Build up a list of local amenities, discounts and special offers available for young people. Some local authorities offer free access to sports facilities for care-experienced young people. Look around for slightly more unusual sports and keep a list of clubs. If time permits, pop into your local judo club or riding school and see what they can offer to the young people with whom you work.
- Find out about local opportunities for volunteering and about schemes such as the Duke of Edinburgh Award. Some young people may be interested in volunteering overseas, so contact organisations such as Voluntary Service Overseas.
- Your local authority may run forums, drops-in and group activities for care-experienced young people, but if not, consider whether this is something you could start up. Make links with local youth work services and organisations like Connexions to find out about other clubs, activities and drop-ins that are on offer.
- Make links with organisations like A National Voice, Voices from Care, Cymru and The Who Cares? Trust to find out about events young people can take part in. There are frequently consultation and training events for care-experienced young people, but there

may also be fun events around arts, craft and drama. For example, NCH runs an annual art weekend called ARTiculation, offering a range of workshops on art, drama, dance, performance poetry, etc, and young people who get really interested can then sign up to take part in future drama performances.

- Recognise that sometimes young people who are living on a small budget will sign up for events even when they aren't particularly interested – they are simply looking for something that's free and offers them a new experience. They may not come away with the skills that a particular course or activity was offering but they have still participated in something new, met new people and probably been in a new environment.

- Look for activities that will motivate young people to have high aspirations. The first Believe in Me Awards (for care-experienced young people to nominate an adult who had made a significant difference to their lives) were held at Claridge's Hotel, London. Everyone was encouraged to dress up for the occasion, the tables were beautifully decorated, and the children and young people were served the same food as the adults. Several celebrities attended – including a major Hollywood star who mingled with the guests. Initially, some workers were concerned that young people would feel overwhelmed or wouldn't eat the food. These worries were proved groundless, and many young people said it was one of the best days of their lives.

- Holding events in a university can be a good way for young people to experience what it's like to live and study on campus – which can be very motivational.

Some of the young people weren't quite sure why they'd come to the media training event on giving radio and TV interviews. Their workers had told them about it and they quite liked the sound of it. But even those who said they'd decided that giving interviews wasn't right for them, gave positive feedback and said they'd learned some new skills and had fun. They'd also enjoyed their day in the

> *city and had loved the chance to be in a really posh hotel.*
>
> *Media Trainer, working with care leavers*

Mentoring

Mentoring takes many different forms – from peer mentoring schemes and schemes where professional adults take young people into their workplaces, through to the simple one-to-one relationship some young people develop with a worker or member of the foster carer's family. Mentors might help young people to gain specific skills or new aspirations, or support them to prepare for specific goals or events, like leaving care. Or they may simply add to the overall quality of a young person's life and range of experiences and motivate them to aim for more in their lives.

Research by York University (*Mentoring young people leaving care: someone for me*, Jasmine Clayden and Mike Stein, Joseph Rowntree Foundation, 2005) carried out in 14 care leaver mentoring projects supported by The Prince's Trust found some positive outcomes from mentoring, such as:

- young people felt mentoring offered them a type of relationship that was different from both professional help and support provided by their families
- young people who had been mentored for over a year were more likely to have achieved goals and made some plans for the future. Two-fifths of the young people had made some future plans.

> *It's not because they take you out or anything like that. It's because they explain things in a better way than professionals would. They help you to cope with certain situations.*
>
> *Danielle, from 'Mentoring young people leaving care: someone for me,' by Jasmine Clayden and Mike Stein, published by the Joseph Rowntree Foundation, 2005*

Gilligan cites a range of research which indicates that mentoring has a range of benefits for young people. 'Considering mentoring in all its forms (formal or 'natural'), *Rhodes et al* (2006) propose that mentors may contribute to the social and emotional, cognitive and identity development of the young person, and that the quality of the relationship may be influenced by factors such as the young person's previous attachments, the level of sensitive "attachment" to the young person achieved by the mentor in the relationship, and the duration of the relationship' ('Spare time activities for young people in care: what can they contribute to educational progress', Robbie Gilligan, *Adoption & Fostering*, 32:1, p. 97, 2007).

This suggests there is a lot more to a mentor/mentee relationship than simply pairing up a young person with someone who seems to fit the bill on paper. A mutual interest in cycling or Manga cartoons may help to establish the relationship, but equally, a young person might bond with someone whose temperament and manner is most appealing to them. A shy young person may be more confident paired with a quieter, more reserved mentor or alternatively may embrace the opportunity to be with someone who is naturally outward going and confident. In other words – it's all about the time spent establishing what is important to the young person and then helping the relationship to develop.

- Find out about local mentoring schemes or, if time and resources permit, think about ways your local authority or organisation could set up such a scheme. The Prince's Trust provides free tools and assessment guidelines for organisations setting up care leavers mentoring schemes. Rainer also runs schemes to help recruit and establish both adult and peer mentors for young people.
- Mentoring schemes should do the preparation, CRB checks and others aspects of preparing mentors. They will probably have their own methods of matching and introducing young people to mentors. Remember that you know more about the young person than they do and you may be better suited to pick up mismatches or issues which are less obvious to someone who doesn't know the young person particularly well. So aim to work collaboratively with colleagues running the mentoring scheme. You may also be best placed to recommend ways of introducing the young person to the mentor which the project may not have considered.

- Help young people to get the best out of their mentor. Ask about the progress of the relationship, how they're coping with the regular meetings and offer suggestions and support to resolve any problems. Research published in *Mentoring young people leaving care* found that half of the mentoring relationships in the study had some negative outcomes, which were often linked to the young people's chaotic lifestyles. In a fifth of such cases, the mentors withdrew.

- Don't overlook the value of informal mentoring relationships. Young people in care may lose more than carers or friends when they move schools or placements. They may also lose a valuable mentoring relationship established with a teacher, dinner lady, member of the foster family, a key worker, youth club leader, etc, so be sure you can help them identify relationships that are meaningful to them.

The following example... concerns a young boy, John, in a residential unit who loved nothing more than to spend time in the kitchen helping to bake cakes. He had interest and ability, and also thrived in the one-to-one attention involved in baking with the particular care worker. John was not a star at school and still struggled to read. But as he got more interested in baking and cooking he saw that his mentor used cookery books a lot and he soon wanted to be able to read the recipes so that he too could deliver successful results. With this stimulus, John quickly became a more motivated student and a more proficient reader.

Taken from 'Spare time activities for young people in care: what can they contribute to educational progress', by Robbie Gilligan, *Adoption & Fostering*, 32:1, p. 97, 2007

Education and development never end

Education is a lifelong process, and while it's important to encourage young people to make the best of educational opportunities while they are still at school, we need to recognise that some will not be ready or able to go to college or university at the usual age. Changes are being made to legislation in recognition of the fact that care leavers may choose to attend college or university a few years later than the majority of young people. However, there is still pressure on them to undertake higher education before they are 25.

Remember that people can return to studying later in life. Some young people may be so concerned about earning their own living in order to support themselves that they will want to train for practical skills or get a job as early as possible. This doesn't mean they are not interested in further education, and they may plan to study full or part time once they feel more financially secure and able to fund this for themselves.

Encourage young people to take an open and active interest in learning opportunities of all kinds and see themselves as "lifelong learners". The system may be inclined to write off young people who have not achieved their academic potential by their mid-20s, but for some young people the skills they learn from managing difficult life situations at an early age, and the maturity and insight this gives them, will equip them to make a success of their lives. NVQs and initiatives to encourage more mature adults without formal qualifications into certain professions may create opportunities they could not access at an earlier age.

TIP 6

Ensure young people have practical skills for young adult life

A young person who'd grown up in a residential unit told me he'd no idea how light bulbs got replaced. As far as he was concerned, the janitor did something with a ladder – but he didn't know about the existence of light bulbs as things you bought in packets and changed until he started living by himself. Many of the everyday things you or I take for granted were a complete mystery – he didn't

> *know how washing machines worked, how food got bought or how you put out the rubbish.*
>
> *Young People's Involvement Worker*

With the best will in the world, a busy residential worker or foster carer may not be able to spend the necessary time with a young person to make sure they properly absorb the knowledge and skills they'll need for running their own home. Or, the worker or carer may assume that the young person has some basics in place. So part of your role in preparing a young person for adult living is to ensure they have appropriate skills – for example, practical skills like cooking and cleaning, and personal skills to negotiate relationships and safeguard their health and well-being. (Budgeting skills are covered in a separate chapter.)

Don't assume young people understand how things work

Watching a young person progressing to the highest level of a computer game, you could be forgiven for assuming they have a sound knowledge of all things to do with IT. And while they may know how to programme the DVD or access MySpace, they may not know how to use a keyboard or send an email. It is estimated that 25 million people in the UK do not use the internet, and young people form a significant proportion of that number.

- Encourage young people to draw up lists of the things they think they will need for their new home and discuss these with them. This will help you to get a feel of their awareness of how a household operates and gaps in their knowledge.
- Consider investing in copies of *Getting sorted!* and *Getting more sorted!* (by Rebecca Davidson, BAAF, 2006), which contain checklists to help young people prepare for moving. They also contain information on a broad range of topics to help young people prepare for young adult living, including physical and emotional health and living with other people.
- Try to arrange some practical sessions for young people or find

local organisations that offer them – e.g. in basic computing, DIY, painting and decorating, first aid.

Ensure young people understand the basics of food and cookery

- Consider asking a local restaurant if their chefs will do a cookery demonstration for young people. Suggest they cook something interesting but relatively simple.
- Ensure that young people understand concepts like sell-by, best before and use-by dates, so they don't throw out food unnecessarily or eat food that has gone off.
- Build up a collection of simple recipes that you can photocopy and give to young people. Encourage them to look out for cheap cookery books in charity shops and car boot sales.
- Encourage young people to look up recipes on the internet and visit the cookery section of the library. They can also pick up tips from television cookery programmes.
- Encourage foster carers and key workers to provide opportunities for young people to plan, shop for and cook meals.
- Some young people may be interested in getting involved in the production of food – there may be a local allotment or organic project which already runs sessions for young people. If not, establish some links with relevant projects and explore options for young people to visit the allotments and help to grow and cook the produce.

Don't assume young people know how to stay healthy

Young people in care may have been subjected to a considerable number of health checks and assessments as they moved in or out of care or between placements. They may have attended sessions with counsellors or therapists. If they have disabilities, they may have spent time in hospital or attended regular outpatient appointments. For some, it may seem that their health has become a matter of public property, something which other people monitor and record – like so many aspects of their lives in the care system. For them, becoming independent may present itself as an opportunity to get away from appointments and procedures which they considered to be intrusive.

How, therefore, can you encourage them to take full responsibility for their own health and well-being once they become young adults?

Most young people pick up basic information about exercise, healthy eating, relationships, contraception and sexual health as part of their schooling. However, if a young person has missed out or been unable to concentrate for large parts of their time at school, they may be lacking some of that knowledge.

Don't assume young people have basic information, but, on the other hand, avoid simply teaching them facts. Instead, try to get them thinking about these issues through discussions or quizzes. What do they understand by "five a day" in terms of fruit and vegetables? Do tinned foods count, why is fibre important in our diets, or what happens if you skip breakfast?

Build up a library of accessible resources. The Who Cares? Trust publishes a handy ring binder book called *Who Cares? About health*, which is designed to be highly accessible to children and young people. It covers a wide range of topics including healthy eating, exercise, skincare and staying healthy, through to emotional health, sexuality, sexual health, drugs and alcohol.

Encourage young people to find information for themselves and discuss it with their peers. You can use this as an opportunity to help them develop some debating skills at the same time. Suggest some topics for debate, such as 'Can you take too much exercise?'

Don't assume that every very thin girl or boy has an eating disorder – some people are just naturally thin. Remember that overeating and binge eating are also disorders, and some prescription drugs can lead to weight loss or weight gain. So don't jump to conclusions before you have more evidence about the young person's eating patterns, and avoid simplistic messages about healthy eating and weight loss or gain.

Be aware of sensitivities around eating disorders and the issues associated with body image. Look out for useful information on sites such as www.b-eat.co.uk run by the Eating Disorders Association, which provides information for professionals, families and young people.

When giving advice or information to young people about healthy eating, try to focus on the need to fuel our bodies with the right balance of foods rather than have discussions about what makes people fat or thin. Remember to include messages about moderation, as young people may have got into distorted patterns of thinking – e.g. 'It's never OK to eat chocolate or chips' or 'It's OK to eat chocolate and chips every day because I never put on weight.'

Ensure young people understand how important it is to get on the list of an NHS dentist. You might want to do this by finding some article – or encouraging them to do their own research – about dentists' waiting lists in some parts of the UK.

Encourage young people to make informed decisions around sex and sexual health

> *Everyone talks about condoms, but when I got pregnant I didn't know there were other ways you could get contraception which could've been better for me. I love my babies, but I wish I'd been a bit older.*
>
> Care leaver and parent

Here are some ideas for ensuring that young people receive relevant and accessible information about sex and sexual health.

- Don't assume that all young women who have been in care will become pregnant at an early age – but recognise that there is a higher statistical likelihood of this. Ensure that messages about contraception are delivered in ways that respect young women. Emphasise their ability to choose whether or not to become pregnant. (More about parenthood can be found in the chapter on Tip 10.)
- Recognise that some young people will have received mixed messages about sexuality and sexual health. They may not realise they have the right to say no to sex or that condoms are not always 100 per cent safe. Helping young people to build self-esteem and value themselves as sexual beings who have choices

can be much more productive than any moralising or scare-mongering about sexual health.

- Ensure you have a range of information about different methods of contraception and protection from socially transmitted diseases and can talk knowledgeably about these. Find out which local clinics or drop-in services provide information and advice specifically for young people.

- Provide sexual education in the context of helping young people recognise their emotions and understand relationships. Young people with learning disabilities or young people whose emotional development has been affected by trauma may have problems identifying their emotions and need support to do this. For example, they may not be able to connect warning feelings like "butterflies in your stomach" with emotions around anxiety and fear.

- Don't assume that young people with learning disabilities have received enough information about sexuality and relationships. Young people with learning disabilities may need support to recognise the difference between private and public areas of the body and between consensual and non-consensual sex.

- Don't concentrate just on young women. Many care-experienced young men become fathers at an early age. Ensure they have the knowledge to make informed choices about this.

There are some very useful resources for workers and young people which can be found on the Making Choices Keeping Safe website (www.mcks.scots.nhs.uk) run by Lothian NHS. Publications include the "stories without words series" produced by the Royal College of Psychiatrists. Titles include *Keeping Healthy "Down Below", Hug Me Touch Me* and *Falling in Love*. Some helpful resources for workers published by Barnardo's include *Meeting the personal and sexual relationship needs of children and young adults with a learning disability*.

Books and films can be powerful ways to stimulate discussion about sexual activity. Melvin Burgess's powerful novels for young people, *Doing It* and *Lady: My life as a bitch*, pull no punches but have enough salacious details to tempt even the most reluctant reader!

Ensure young people have opportunities to make informed choices about alcohol and drugs

Some young people will have been personally affected by drugs and alcohol – either having a problem themselves or experiencing inappropriate drug and alcohol use in their families, which may have resulted in them coming into the care system. Be careful to deliver messages in ways which recognise this and are supportive rather than simplistic.

Encourage young people to do their own research and have lively and stimulating discussions about drugs and alcohol. A discussion about the types of advertising messages which work or don't work can be a better way of engaging young people in debates than simply presenting "a session about drugs/alcohol".

The Who Cares? Trust produces a colourful ring-bound book for children and young people called *Who Cares? About drugs*. It includes explanations of why people may use drugs and issues around dependency, information about drugs, the law, what to do in an emergency and how to support someone who has a drug problem.

Young people are more likely to listen to their peers on issues around drugs and alcohol. Arrange opportunities for young people to meet with former drug users or people who have had serious alcohol problems who can talk about the realities of living with these problems. Avoid using anyone who is too evangelical, but look for speakers who are honest, open and able to highlight the downsides in ways which will be relevant to young people.

Again, books and films can be powerful ways to stimulate discussion. The hard-hitting *Junk* and *Smack* by Melvin Burgess are used in a number of schools for this purpose. The book *Trainspotting* by Irvine Walsh may be more appealing for Scottish young people or the keen reader who is prepared to struggle with an unfamiliar dialect, but the film *Trainspotting* (1996, Danny Boyce) may be more accessible for a wider audience. However, some viewers find the film too graphic, so it may be unsuitable for more sensitive young people.

The website www.talktofrank.com offers an A–Z of drugs, their properties and side effects. It also provides sources of support and young people's stories. Some professionals and young people have commented on the fact that this seemingly neutral information service has become too explicit in its anti-drug messages, and this has alienated some people from using the site.

> *Sometimes you have to help young people make the connections. If they get arrested for drug possession, they may not be able to travel to and live in other countries, which can really mess up their future plans.*
>
> *Young People's Empowerment Worker*

Encourage young people to develop emotional health and healthy relationships

> *Going to the gym and looking after your physical health is important. So is talking to someone about how you feel. Getting support to stay emotionally healthy should be seen as good as going to the gym three times a week – it should be respected. Jas, 18.*
>
> *Taken from www.youngminds.org.uk*

Encourage young people to talk about their feelings and develop emotional literacy, as these can be powerful ways of helping them to become emotionally resilient. You could also introduce them to different approaches to life which will open their eyes to other ways of behaving or regarding the world. Some schools teach children basic concepts of transactional analysis (TA) and TA is also taught to some social workers, foster carers, etc. TA is based on a philosophy of mutual respect and a belief in everyone's ability to learn and change. It can help children gain insights into how previous experiences affect people's feelings and thinking – so they can, for example, make conscious choices about how they interact with others or view the world in the future.

Young people you work with may have feelings of sadness or depression, or may experience depressive illness or, in some cases, mental illness. Try to keep yourself informed about current research into these issues, the differences between them, and the best ways to support young people going through these experiences.

Not all these issues require professional intervention, but it is important to know what services are available locally or through websites, and to think about the most tactful and supportive ways to encourage young people to get help.

The Young Minds website is a good source of information about promoting mental health and responding to concerns. It produces materials for professionals on topics such as Child and Adolescent Mental Health Services (CAMHS), depression and bullying, and has a wealth of online and printed resources for young people. Some of its resources are free.

The Royal College of Psychiatrists website (www.rcpsych.ac.uk) offers a range of information on topics such as obsessive compulsive disorder in young people, self-harm and many other mental health issues. Its leaflet for workers and carers titled *'Depression in People with Learning Disabilities'* can also be viewed on the website.

When I was younger I was pushed around a lot by other people. These days I know my mind and what I want. I like to live somewhere clean and tidy. I'm fussy about it. When I moved into my new place, the other people there were such scruffs. It made me so mad. I used to tell them I wouldn't put up with it. I wrote a list of rules but no-one followed them. I even got into a fight with one of the girls about it.

My boyfriend told me I was stressing too much. He said I should try and see it from other people's point of view. We had a house meeting and I said what I felt. Other people said what they felt. We came up

> *with some rules everyone said they'd follow. It's not perfect but it works OK. I get less stressed now if someone forgets to wash up.*
>
> *From 'Getting More Sorted' by Rebecca Davidson, BAAF, 2006, p. 26*

Developing social skills

Young people develop ways of interacting with the world based on their past experiences. They may develop entrenched ideas about how things should be, and this may lead, at times, to behaviour that gets negative reactions from other people. Young people also tend to pick up messages from the media about what is acceptable behaviour – for example, they may start to believe that the heated interactions between characters in soap operas are the only way to behave.

Getting more sorted! (by Rebecca Davidson, BAAF, 2006) has a section about living with other people – with particular emphasis on preparing to move into shared accommodation. It aims to help young people recognise the potential benefits of being able to get along with others and has tips about avoiding unnecessary conflict.

Encourage young people to recognise the validity of their own feelings, but help them understand that sometimes they need to make choices about how they express them.

Some young people are not aware that other people have different perspectives. They may need help to recognise that it's fine to have an opinion, fine to change your mind – and fine to agree to disagree.

Help young people to recognise the difference between asserting their right to a point of view and being blinkered or aggressive. This may be quite difficult if they have had to stick up for themselves in abusive situations, as it may challenge deeply held views which have seen them through very difficult times. TA, as mentioned earlier, has lots of accessible exercises that help people identify different "drivers" or approaches to life. Young people are often fascinated to discover that their personal approach to life – such as a tendency to "Be Strong, Be

Perfect, Please People" isn't the only way to be, and that every approach has both positives and negatives that can work most effectively when combined with people who have different positives and negatives.

Tactics: transactional analysis concepts for all trainers, teachers and tutors plus insight into collaborative learning strategies (by Rosemary Napper and Trudi Newton, 2000, published by TA Resources) is a practical resource geared for work with children and young people. For information, visit www.taresources.co.uk.

Encourage young people to think about different ways they could behave in a situation. Working on fictional situations – for example, discussing characters in a soap opera or film – may be an easier place to start than focusing on an issue personal to them.

When a young person is very upset, it's not always helpful to immediately start asking them what they could have done differently. Give them some time to get the issues off their chest so they will be prepared to listen and realise that you are supportive. It is usually best to wait until they have calmed down a bit before you encourage them to think about how they might have done things differently or what would have resulted from a different course of action.

TIP 7

Enable young people to get the best out of their budget and avoid debts

How many of us really budget as well as we should? When we do overspend, we can reach for our credit card or use an overdraft facility. Yet the system expects young people who may never have had to manage their own money to budget effectively, plan for the future and stay out of debt.

As a worker you can ensure that the young people you work with develop some essential budgeting skills – although you may need to start by polishing up your own first.

Polish up your own budgeting skills

> *At any age you can have an account opened in your name with a bank or building society. Providing they think you understand the nature of transactions, you can operate the account yourself. Under-18s cannot have an overdraft...*
>
> *'From age seven you can draw money from a Post Office account.*
>
> From 'Getting Sorted' by Rebecca Davidson, BAAF, 2006, p. 120

Just how good are your own budgeting skills? How much do you really know about opening a first bank account or taking out a contract for a mobile phone? Do you always read the small print before you sign any form of financial agreement? How do you get the best deals in the supermarket or ensure you have enough money to pay your bills each month, and how would you explain this to a young person?

Taking a good look at your own budgeting skills and knowledge of basic financial matters can be a good starting point for anyone preparing to pass these skills on to young people. The Citizens Advice Bureaux and Connexions provide advice and information about money matters. The Financial Services Agency (FSA) (the UK's financial watchdog) produces a range of leaflets about many aspects of budgeting and being a consumer (information about this can be found on their website).

At the time of publication, the FSA was running a free one-day training course for professionals working with young people. Begun in 2006, it aims to train 20,000 youth workers by the end of 2010. The Young People and Money Programme is managed by LifeLine and delivered across the UK by A4e, Citizens Advice Northern Ireland, Fairbridge and LifeLine – all organisations specialising in work with young people who are "Not in Education,

Employment or Training (NEET)".

Young people need to learn basic budgeting skills

> *They tell you that you need to budget, but they don't tell you how to do this. You need trial runs to the shops.*
>
> Joy, ex-care leaver

Some schools include budgeting skills as part of the curriculum, but that does not mean young people will have paid attention or even understood the relevance of this to their own lives. Like many skills in life, budgeting is best learned by getting hands-on practice in a supportive environment.

It's also important to help young people make links between skills like budgeting and their future life. Young people who are disengaged with education may see budgeting skills as just one more lesson that they know they're going to find boring. Learning about money doesn't have to be serious stuff and the more fun the young person has with it, the more likely they are to pick up useful information.

Asking a young person to compare prices on the internet for the top-of-the-range car they eventually hope to own or the holiday they want to take may be a good way of creating some basic awareness, which you and the young person can then build on.

Link budgeting with practical skills

A young person is unlikely to be able to shop economically if they have no idea what to cook or what sort of products they need for keeping the house clean. Providing written information can be very helpful, but as some of the best learning usually occurs when people can experience something first hand, try to offer experiential learning opportunities.

Back-up written information is always helpful, but is most effective when used as part of a conversation or as a reminder of what someone has already learned. Rather than reinvent the wheel with each young person, create and update your own information pack which you can photocopy and give to the young people with whom you work. It is also useful to consider providing all care leavers with copies of *Getting Sorted* and *Getting More Sorted*, by Rebecca Davidson. These books are written for young people leaving care and include lots of practical advice and checklists.

- Encourage the young person to create a list of basic household cleaning products. Which ones are essential and which are nice to have if you can afford them?
- Take young people to the supermarket. This provides a good opportunity to talk about the process and discover how much they know about budgeting.
- Don't assume young people know even basic information. Encourage them to become a canny consumer, for example by:
  - writing a shopping list and attempting to stick to it
  - looking out for two-for-one offers (but only if this is something they really need)
  - not assuming that named brands are always the best
  - looking out for opportunities to bulk buy cheaply
  - recognising that loose goods may be cheaper than packaged goods.
- Some supermarkets sell very cheap calculators. You could get a supply of these to give out to young people, and encourage them to add things up as they go around the shop.
- Create some challenges and competitions young people can take part in. Looking for the best value washing powder in the shopping mall isn't much fun until you do it against the clock or against one of your mates. Make sure you don't annoy the shop staff, so put boundaries around behaviour – you don't want to get yourself and the young people thrown out for being a nuisance. Buying the prizes – e.g. chocolate bars – may be a good way to end the visit, and keep the store staff happy.
- Make sure young people are aware that not all supermarkets are the same – and be prepared to explain which ones might be more or less expensive. Be aware that young people who have moved out of their home area may be familiar with a supermarket chain

that isn't available in your part of the country, so may need you to help them find a comparable one.

- Ensure that young people know about "pound shops" and the bargains to be had from market stalls.
- Provide suggestions and details about places where young people can get bargain furniture and household items – e.g. local auctions, some supermarkets, closing down sales, etc.

Encourage young people to plan ahead and anticipate the unexpected

Have you ever had one of those months when you think you're doing quite well with managing your finances, when out of the blue the fridge stops working, your car breaks down, the washing machine mangles your only smart pair of trousers, and you suddenly realise you haven't bought your best friend a birthday present? Hopefully, you will have a reserve of money you can call upon to help you through those difficult times, or if not, you will reach for your credit card to see you through. For all of us, life is unpredictable and we can never be prepared for all eventualities. How then can we expect young people to be prepared for those hidden expenses that may suddenly present themselves?

It is a good idea to encourage young people to get into the habit of thinking and planning ahead. Ask them to think about their current situation: how do they spend pocket money or money they earn from a Saturday job? What expenses do they plan for each month – e.g. bus fares, mobile phone card, school meals, etc? How much money do they spend on clothes and going out with friends? What unexpected expenses have come up recently – or might come up during the months ahead? How are they going to budget for these?

You can also ask young people to imagine the type of expenses they might have when they first start living as a young adult. Then ask them to think about all the extras that might come up. Encourage them to think about things like:

- replacing lost or damaged clothes or household items
- extras they may need for a hair cut, new clothes for a job interview
- what happens if they lose money or someone steals from them

- how they will budget for times like Christmas or other significant festivals, and for things like birthdays and anniversaries
- what might be the best way of keeping money for emergencies.

Be aware of additional support young people may be entitled to

Up to 18:
A local authority has a statutory duty to provide financial support to young people in public care until they reach the age of 18. The weekly living allowance should never be less than the amount a person of that age would be entitled to from benefits. However, guidance enables local authorities to make additional payments, and local authorities can be creative in their approach to this. For example, some elected members have an allocated budget to pay for driving lessons or vouchers for DIY and furniture stores for care leavers.

Each local authority should provide a statement of support spelling out the financial support it will provide to care leavers. It may be not be easy to locate your authority's statement or to persuade the local authority responsible for the care leaver to do so.

Over 18
Once a young person reaches 18 and is no longer in education, the local authority is not obliged to support them financially. They must claim benefits if they cannot support themselves. However, young people over 18 may be entitled to additional help such as:

- a payment from the local authority/trust for something like a rent deposit or to cover shortfalls in housing benefits (these are often discretionary and you will need to help the young person make a good case for receiving this money)
- community care grants to pay for furniture, moving costs, connection charges, clothes, etc (these are non-repayable)
- crisis loans, which are sometimes available for people who are entitled to community care grants
- budgeting loans to cover things such as rent in advance or household items. These are available to most people who have been on Income Support or Jobseeker's Allowance for 26 weeks and are paid back through deductions from the person's benefits.

Young people with disabilities may be able to claim benefits at 17, for example, the Disability Living Allowance.

In Scotland, students may be able to claim a care leaver's grant through the Student Award Agency Scotland.

Care leavers are entitled to help with health costs.

Help young people prepare for the transition from allowances to adult living

As a good corporate parent, your local authority needs to think about its responsibilities towards young people. Paying young people a generous allowance when they are 16 and 17 may be well intentioned, but what happens when the young person turns 18 and finds they have to live on benefits or a low-paid job? This is an issue that local authorities probably need to consider at policy level (e.g. considering measures such as paying into a Children's Trust Fund – within the legal limits), but as their worker you can also play a key role in helping young people to prepare for different financial circumstances.

> *My local authority was very good to me when I was at college and that, but I remember the first day I got a bill! I was like – how do they expect me to pay this! It's important that you prepare young people for when they are going to have to pay their own way – otherwise it comes as a big shock. One day you have all this money you are given and then you have a birthday and then it's all down to you to. . . You've had all this money and then it's not there any more.*
>
> *Ex-care leaver*

How can you create awareness in young people that their financial situation may change quite radically when they become 18 (or older if they are in education) – without scaring them? Maybe you can arrange for them to meet with ex-care leavers who can talk to them about this.

How can you encourage young people to put aside money or buy items for the future? Again, it may be worth calling on the support of older care leavers who have experienced this for themselves.

Help young people with disabilities to get the best out of their allowances

The system surrounding disability benefits is a complex one and unless you have worked in the field before, you may find yourself struggling to make sense of it.

However, you should not allow a personal lack of knowledge to make you complacent. It can be all too easy to think 'The disability team has already sorted this out'; or to assume that the foster carer is the expert on benefits; or to be ready to believe the young person when they tell you that 'Everything has been done' to ensure they have all the benefits they are entitled to. The young person – or their carer – may have received inaccurate information from other people.

Benefits advisers don't always get things right and the law and circumstances change. You may also find that although the young person has a good social care support package in place, they may not be receiving any advice about the financial benefits they are entitled to.

It can be a good idea to seek advice from an experienced benefits adviser, from a local disability organisation or other advice centre, depending on what is available locally. This advice worker should do an audit of what the young person is receiving already and any possible other claims that could be made.

Wherever possible, try to involve key members of the young person's support network in discussions about this issue, and get as much clarity as possible about what the young person is already receiving. Through a detailed discussion, you are most likely to be able to identify any loopholes or opportunities for change. For example, changes in circumstance may mean that the young person is entitled to new or revised benefits – and this may not come to light until it is considered in detail. Your work with the young person may have brought to light needs, interests and career aspirations that other people know nothing about.

The current thrust of social care policy is towards empowering individuals to make choices for themselves rather than slot into existing provision. To do this, more and more people will be given individual budgets to spend as they – and, where appropriate, their carers and support workers – see fit. This form of "self directed support" includes people employing their own care staff. It also encompasses possibilities such as individuals deciding that their needs for social contact can be better met by paying a friend or neighbour to take them to a sports club, cinema or pub, instead of attending a traditional day centre. With these new options come new challenges, for example, how will a young person ensure they are a "good employer" of their care worker? Or how will a young person ensure they spend money wisely when they have little or no experience of budgeting and have possibly been "over-protected" in the earlier stages of their life?

These issues all need careful consideration and you are advised to tap into the work that is already being done in this area. For example, the In Control project in England, Scotland and Wales is pioneering good practice around self-directed support – see www.in-control.org.uk.

Help young people with the paperwork

Offer some initial help with filling in forms for things like Income Support and ensure young people have the phone numbers of relevant departments to contact. Where time permits, accompany them on their first visit.

Tenancy agreements, contracts, bank statements and bills can be very confusing for young people who have never had to deal with them before. Make some time to ensure they understand these documents and have understood the implications involved. Encourage young people to do some research before entering into any type of contract and to ensure they have understood things like cancellation policies.

Setting up a bank account can be baffling, so spend some time helping young people think through their needs rather than simply opting for banks that give the best incentives. Ensure that young people understand basic concepts like "current account" and "deposit account" and the difference between debit and credit cards.

Prevent young people getting into serious debt

It is inevitable that some young people – whatever their family circumstances – will end up in debt. This can be a useful learning experience but only if there are enough safeguards around to ensure it doesn't escalate out of control. Ensure that the young people you work with know how to access help at an early stage – and recognise the need to do so.

Don't wait until a problem occurs, but ensure that right from the start they have details of organisations like Citizens Advice Bureaux and government-funded debt counselling services, so they will be less tempted to take out expensive loans or call some of the commercial debt helplines they see advertised on television. Stockpile useful leaflets and spend time looking at these with young people to ensure they have understood the information.

> *One of our care leavers, who is 21, came to us because he had got into some serious rent arrears. We didn't tell him he was too old for our help. We didn't even signpost him to someone who could help him. We paid his rent arrears. OK, to be fair we didn't just hand him the cash. We did what any responsible parent would do and insisted that he do some work to pay us back... We also spoke to him (or nagged him, as he may describe it) about budgeting and coming to us before things go too far – after all, we can't help if we don't know. Our housing staff have helped and supported him back into education and I've persuaded him to get involved with some work I'm doing. His CV is going to look very healthy this time next year, so long term we've done more than pay his rent arrears.*

Hopefully we've made a difference to his longer-term future too.

Benni-Jo Tyler, Young People's Involvement Worker for Shaftesbury Young People

TIP 8

Support young people to find housing and access benefits

It really helps when people can do little bits and pieces for you because the local authority system is so complicated – and even people who work there don't always know what's available.

Ex-care leaver, 24

If your own son or daughter was preparing to move into their own accommodation, would you simply hand them a contact list and tell them to get on with it? Life is a complex business, so why should we expect that preparing a young person for adult living is something that can be undertaken by just one worker?

Getting the balance right between encouraging young people to start acting independently and providing some hand-holding through some of the more challenging stages can be tricky. However, if you support young people in the early stages, so that their confidence grows through the process, they are more likely to take more steps on their own in the future.

Ensure young people have a chance to think through the options and make changes if required

> *Pathway Plans must always be flexible so that young people can change their minds about things like where to live or what job to do. It's a natural thing to do. How many of us can look back and say yes, I'm living in exactly the kind of house I planned when I was 16 or doing the sort of job I had in mind when I chose my "O" levels?*
>
> *Young People's Support Worker*

While creating the Pathway Plan, a young person may be adamant that they want their own place when they reach 17. However, the young person then chooses to stay with their foster carers while they finish their A levels. They then decide to go to college, and want to share a house with a group of friends. Are your ways of working flexible and responsive enough to support young people as their needs change, and to recognise times when young people may be having second thoughts about earlier decisions?

We should not expect young people to stick with a decision simply because it has been written into their Pathway Plan. As their life experiences broaden, they become aware of a wider range of options open to them and may identify their own needs and strengths and areas where they need some support. You can play a very important role by ensuring that they are able to make housing choices which reflect their personal situations and their priorities.

- Help young people to realise that adults change their minds in the light of new evidence. Some young people may have taken on board messages about "being indecisive" or "not knowing their own minds" and may believe that once you make a decision you have to stick with it.

- Ensure young people are aware of new options that may become available. A young person may have heard negative things about the independent living unit provided by your local authority or trust and not want to move there, but unbeknownst to them the service has been revamped or is now provided by an outside agency. It might be worth suggesting a visit so they are at least aware of this as one of several possibilities. Present such visits as opportunities for them to see the full range of options available, otherwise they may suspect you are trying to twist their arm and they may become resistant.

- Help young people to identify their own priorities and to be clear where they are or are not prepared to make compromises. For example, if a young person is absolutely clear they will only live by themselves or is adamant about going to live with an older sibling, help them to identify the reasons why they are saying this. They may be working on assumptions which are out of date or they may have forgotten to factor in some relevant issues. Only by helping them to be absolutely clear with themselves about why they are thinking in a particular way, can you encourage them to consider pitfalls or other options.

- Be clear about what is and what is not good enough for the corporate child of your local authority – and encourage decision makers and budget holder to do the same. Would they be happy for their children to live in a damp bedsit?

- What about holiday accommodation for young people who live on campus during term time? Would you be happy for your own child to stay with a different family every holiday or for your disabled child to spend their holidays in a residential unit with much older people? If holiday periods are a misery for a young person in education, they may be tempted to give up their education. Try to find creative solutions such as enabling the young person to return to their foster family, to develop an ongoing relationship with people who can provide supported lodgings or, if this is not possible for a particular holiday period, what about paying for them to go travelling or take part in a residential course they'll really enjoy? Or simply ensure that the young person is in receipt of sufficient money to stay on campus during holiday periods or to pay a retainer for their belongings to remain on campus? You could also explore ways in which the money for holiday accommodation and living could be kept separate from term-time expenses – as it can be tempting for students to dip into the extra money on the assumption they will be able to find a job during the holidays, and this may not be the case.

I would like to have a trial to see if I can handle moving out, or if I want it. That way I have the choice to go back home if I can't cope.

Young person, from 'Care Matters Consultation Responses', DfES, 2007

- If a young person seems very uncertain about moving or seems to have highly unrealistic expectations about how things will be, is there any way they could have a trial period of moving out of care to see if they are ready for it? This may not be easy to arrange, but try to be creative in providing opportunities. Are there any supported lodgings-type carers who can let out a room to a young person for a short while, treating them as if they are simply a lodger but being ready to offer support if it is needed.
- Familiarise yourself with the type of accommodation available to young people so you can explain it to them. If your local authority or trust contracts services from a "preparation for independence unit" run by a voluntary organisation, have you visited it and can you describe the facilities in detail? Do you know any of the approved families who provide supported lodgings for your local authority? If not, can you make time to meet a few of them?
- Make sure you and other colleagues are aware of the impact of

heavily subsidising accommodation for young people who must later manage on benefits – you may not be doing them a favour in the long run. There have been cases where young people have been forced to leave the accommodation they have enjoyed while they were under 18 or still in education, because the housing and benefits system does not consider them eligible to receive the amount of money needed to pay the rent.

Key findings from the executive summary of *There's no place like home, a survey of care leavers, housing professionals, leaving care workers and personal advisers,* published in 2005 by A National Voice

Young people:

55% felt they had no real choice in the accommodation offered to them

29% did not feel safe in their accommodation

32% felt their accommodation did not meet their needs

50% felt that housing departments were not aware of the particular needs and circumstances of young care leavers

11% were staying with friends

12% were living in a bed & breakfast or hostel accommodation

Housing professionals:

88% felt that young care leavers found it difficult to manage their rent and other finances

55% had not received any training or information on the needs of young care leavers

45% felt their own department did not provide enough support for young care leavers

---

Leaving care professionals:

77% felt that young people were still leaving care at too young an age and without adequate preparation

71% felt there was insufficient attention paid to emotional support for young care leavers

81% agreed that poverty has a negative impact on young care leavers – particularly the constraint it places on their ability to develop social networks or take part in activities

92% had experienced young care leavers being evicted or threatened with eviction and over half of these believed that lack of support had contributed to the situation

Ensuring young people get access to housing

Sometimes a split seems to exist between the local authority housing department and staff supporting and preparing care leavers for young adult life. Staff from these departments may know little about one another's roles and may even give contradictory messages about what a young person is entitled to.

● Make sure you understand how your local housing system works to ensure that the young people you work with have the very best chance of finding accommodation. Not only will you be able to ensure they are accessing the best options to gain the housing they want, but you will also create a foundation for most effective working with housing staff.

● Take the time to make links with your housing department. Do not assume they have a particular understanding of the needs of care-experienced young people – they deal with many different client groups who are all considered a "priority need" and have pressures and targets of their own to meet. It may seem harsh to you that young people are evicted from accommodation by their corporate parent, but you will not be helping anyone if you simply criticise colleagues for doing this, without attempting to increase their understanding of the reasons why care-experienced young people have rent arrears or have problems with their tenancies.

- Try to make time to take young people along to initial meetings with the housing department. Ensure that young people understand the system and how to help themselves to get the type of housing they want. Many councils offer a first-come-first-served system for people who are on equal priority ranking, so young people need to understand that they must put time and effort into looking for the type of accommodation they want.
- Ensure young people have access to ways of finding accommodation – e.g. access to newspapers, council housing websites, etc. Try to accompany young people on their first visit to the library or internet access project, as they may find it difficult to ask for help from staff.
- Ensure young people are able to use the internet to help them in their search for accommodation – never assume all young people are IT literate. Find out about local schemes that offer free internet training, or see if the young person's school or college can offer additional help.
- Put young people in touch with voluntary or community organisations that can help them find accommodation. Their staff may be able to spend more time helping young people make the initial searches for accommodation.
- Try to accompany young people on some of their initial visits to accommodation or ensure that someone like their foster carer or another worker they trust goes with them.
- Help young people to think through in advance the questions they need to ask and what they should be looking out for – you may want to prepare a simple factsheet to help them, for example:
  - Are there any additional charges beyond the rent – e.g. service charges or communal charges?
  - What methods of heating does the accommodation have and is this economical?
  - What is included in the rent – e.g. are heating and electricity separate?
  - If this is shared accommodation, what are the rules – e.g. around cleaning, visitors, preparing food, etc?

Safety issues

Should we be encouraging young people to visit properties on their own? The Suzy Lamplugh Trust has a factsheet about safety issues for anyone letting out or visiting a property, and recommends that people always take someone with them. If this is not possible, they recommend that the person lets others know where they are going and who they are meeting and then contacts them afterwards to let them know they are OK. This guidance sheet, called *Sharing a Flat or House*, also contains information about what safety issues to consider when visiting a property – e.g. visiting at night to see how safe the area feels. It also recommends that people should act on their instincts if they feel that someone would not be a safe person to share with.

Make sure you are sensitive to these issues yourself and don't dismiss young people's concerns, even if they don't feel particularly valid to you. There may be issues in a young person's past that make them feel especially vulnerable which you may not be aware of. If you feel they have a serious problem with trusting strangers or a particularly strong anxiety about being in new places, it may be necessary to refer them to some sort of counselling, e.g. Victim Support, to help them deal with these concerns.

The Suzy Lamplugh Trust also has a range of factsheets on safety issues. They can be downloaded from the website (www.suzylamplugh.org) and may be useful to keep among your resources to give to young people.

Accessing benefits

I was that terrified of forms. I felt sick every time I had to fill one in, I was that scared of making a mistake. I wish I'd got more help with this.

Young person claiming benefits

Young people will only be able to get the best out of the opportunities available to them and to make a success out of living as young adults if they have adequate financial support to do so.

The benefit system is difficult for most adults to understand, so imagine how baffling it must be to a young person who is trying to access it for the first time. Also, young people may have heard stories from friends or relatives about what they are entitled to and been warned that they must stick up for their rights – and so may be tempted to engage with the system in unhelpful ways. Try to accompany young people on their first visit to the Jobcentre or take steps to ensure that someone from another relevant service is doing so. You may also need to help them to fill out forms. Even if they have been the recipients of a lot of form filling during their lives, filling out forms for themselves can make them very anxious.

Never assume someone else has these issues covered. Assisting young people in accessing benefits is one of those tasks which all too often falls between services, so young people end up struggling on their own. If a young person makes a significant mistake – or is tempted to make a false claim – this can have repercussions which will affect the quality of their early adult lives.

Keep yourself abreast of young people's entitlements and any proposed changes to these which may affect the younger age group with which you are working. The Citizens Advice Bureau website (www.adviceguide.org.uk) contains comprehensive information about: benefits for all four nations; obtaining information in different languages; and information about what to do if someone is having problems claiming benefits or wants to challenge a benefit decision.

Staff and local helplines at Citizen Advice Bureaux are a good starting point for workers or young people who have queries about benefit entitlements.

A quick guide to benefits

Apart from in exceptional circumstances, care-experienced young people under 18 are not entitled to claim benefits, and local authorities are expected to support them until their 18th birthday. However, disabled young people may receive benefits at an earlier age.

- **Jobseeker's Allowance** is a benefit for people who are unemployed but capable of work. It is usually only available to over-18s.
- **Income Support** is a benefit to cover day-to-day living costs for

people on a low income. Care-experienced young people aged 16 and 17 are usually not entitled to claim this, but there are some exceptions:

> – lone parents under 18
> – disabled young people.

- **Housing Benefit** and **Council Tax Benefit** enable people on low incomes to pay their rent and council tax. In England and Wales, Council Tax Benefit can only be claimed by people aged 18 or over. Someone under 18 may be eligible to claim Housing Benefit but the amount given to a single person under 25 without children is usually restricted.
- The **Social Fund** helps people on low incomes to pay for one-off expenses, and a young person does not need to be claiming benefit in order to apply.
- If a young person is receiving Income Support or income-based Jobseeker's Allowance, they may also be able to get a **community care grant** or **budgeting loan**.
- **Tax Credits** are means-tested and dependent on income. Young people over 16 may be eligible to claim tax credits.
  To claim Working Tax Credit a young person must:

  > – work 16 hours or more a week
  > – be on a low income
  > – have a disability which affects their ability to get a job
  > – be responsible for a child.

  To claim Child Tax Credit a young person must:

  > – be over 16
  > – be responsible for a child under the age of 16.

  If a young person under 16 has a child, they cannot claim Child Tax Credit in their own right but it can be claimed on their behalf by those with responsibility for the young person.
  Working Tax Credits and Child Tax Credits can be claimed by the parents or carers of a young person under 20 in certain circumstances.
- **Disability benefits**: The system of benefits for young people with disabilities is complex and this book is not going to attempt to explain them for fear of over-simplifying them. If you are working with a disabled young person you may need to obtain additional information to help you understand the young person's existing benefit situation and what benefits they may be entitled

to in the future.

The Department for Work and Pensions has a helpline on benefits for disabled and sick people, their representatives and carers. It is called the Benefits Enquiry Line (BEL) and can be contacted on 0800 882 200. In Northern Ireland, the BEL is run by the Social Security Agency and can be contacted on 0800 220 674. The BEL service can also be contacted by Minicom on 0800 243 355.

The helpline also offers help filling out claim forms over the phone when people are applying for Disability Living Allowance or Attendance Allowance.

You know there are people out there getting all these benefits and you know some of them are working and that... you think, why shouldn't I try to get some of this? Is anyone like me ever going to find out what I should get?'

Young asylum seeker

TIP 9

Support young people to prepare for and make the move as successful as possible

Moving house is recognised as one of the most stressful things we do as human beings – there's so much to organise and so many decisions to make. Sorting through the "stuff" of our lives also brings up many memories – positive and painful, but it's also the time when we start to notice how shabby some of our possessions have become or to start worrying whether we will ever be able to replace that sofa we spilt coffee on.

When young people move into their own home as an adult, it's a very important time for them and it is important for us to ensure it as exciting and positive an experience as possible.

> *My mother collected plates from the local supermarket for about a year before I went to university – it was something like for every three pounds she spent she could buy a dinner plate for 33p, but there were also cups and saucers, and also side plates. Sadly, no bowls – or maybe that offer came later and I missed out. I had everything in brown and orange because that was the colour at the time. Those plates were unbreakable – 30 years later my husband and I are still using some of them. I also had bed linen in the same colour scheme, some of that's still around as well... I took all that for granted, it was just something parents did. But who does that for young people leaving care?*
>
> *Young People's Empowerment Worker*

Getting furniture and equipment for the new place

Make sure you are familiar with your authority's system for dispensing leaving care grants. Amounts can vary hugely between authorities – from a couple of hundred to several thousand, so it's important to be clear how much money the young person will be entitled to. There may also be stipulations about when and how a young person can spend this money, which may affect their ability to start buying items in advance of the move. Once you are familiar with how the system works, make sure that young people are fully aware of it too. They may have met other young people whose local authorities do things differently, and they may be expecting it to be the same for them.

Make sure you are also aware of any additional grants or funding sources young people might be able to access.

Sometimes the less young people have had, the more they feel a need to have things which are new and branded. However, you need to help young people sort out their priorities and recognise that not having the biggest or best of something will enable them to get more for their money and to buy more for their place.

Young people may assume that everyone starts out with a flat screen television, DVD recorder, stereo system and kitchen gadgets because this is what they've seen in their foster carer's home or the homes of people on television. You may need to help them understand that many young people struggle financially when they have their first place and have to find the most economical way to buy furniture and household equipment (unless they are very fortunate) and, importantly, that this is not something exclusively experienced by young people leaving care. Encourage them to prioritise what really matters to them, but recognise that some young people will still make choices you don't agree with.

Getting more sorted has a chapter of tips for preparing to move. It includes checklists of essential items for kitchen, bedroom, bathroom and living room and also a list of "nice but not essential" items. There is also a section about sources of inexpensive furniture, which includes the list below:

● second-hand furniture stores
● car boot sales
● charity shops
● furniture projects (for people on low income)
● auctions (the everyday ones, not the antique ones)
● self-assembly kits from cut-price stores
● unwanted items from friends/family
● "for sale" advertisements in local newspapers/boards in supermarkets and newsagents
● special offers in supermarkets – especially their own brands.

Before the moving day

Getting to know the area

● Hopefully you will have been able to accompany young people on

visits to potential accommodation and helped them think through
the choices, but once the tenancy is signed, suggest going with
them to visit again before they move in.

- Try to spend some time walking around the area with the young
person – visiting local shops, finding locations of bus stops,
locating any local amenities, etc.

- Encourage young people to take opportunities to introduce
themselves to neighbours and local shopkeepers – if appropriate.
Use your discretion and follow the young person's lead on this.
Some young people may be too shy to say "hello" when passing
someone on the stairwell and may appreciate you engaging the
neighbour in a short chat about the neighbourhood. However,
others may resent this and may want to take their own time to
decide whom they choose to talk to.

- If possible, encourage the young person to begin some of the
decorating or take round some of the furniture before they actually
move in, so the new place feels as homely as possible.

Preparing for the move

- If possible, try to spend a little time helping the young person to
decorate or arrange possessions in their new place.

- Help young people to prepare for the move by discussing the
different stages involved – for example, when to contact gas and
electricity suppliers, when to notify the post office of change of
address, and when to arrange delivery of items of furniture.

- Encourage young people to plan carefully for the move itself. Do
they have someone to drive them on the day? Will they need to
hire a van or arrange for someone to collect or deliver large items?
Encourage them to draw up a packing schedule and to pack last
items they need most – so they can get them out first.

- Find out who – if anyone – will be around to support the young
person during the move. Don't assume that other people will do
this. Young people who have good relationships with their foster
carers or key workers may receive plenty of support with the move.
But some foster carers won't have the time to do this, and other
young people may have strained relationships with carers or key
workers.

- Ensure young people have suitcases and suitable containers in which to pack their clothes and treasured possessions. Don't expect young people to pack their possessions in bin bags. Organisations like A National Voice and Voices from Care, Cymru have been campaigning for several years to ensure that no young person moving from any care placement has to pack their possessions in a bin bag for want of a couple of inexpensive suitcases. Moving their clothes and possessions in bin bags can make young people feel devalued and humiliated.

The moving day

- Try to be available on the moving day or ensure young people have someone with them whom they know well and who will help them – e.g. a mentor, foster carer or close friend.
- Encourage young people to pack separately the basics they'll need for the first night, e.g. tea, coffee, bread, toothpaste, towel, etc, in case they are too tired to unpack fully.
- Encourage them to switch the fridge on as early as possible so they can store milk and some easy-cook meals for the first night or two.
- Help or encourage young people to make up their bed as a matter of priority and have some familiar photos and items to hand to put beside the bed.
- Phone or visit later in the day to make sure they are doing OK. Maybe take a little present or send a "welcome to your new home" card. Invest in a stock of these to keep in your desk drawer.
- Encourage the young person to arrange for a close friend to stay with them on their first evening alone.

After the moving day

- Encourage the young person to plan ahead so they have some contact with friends or family to look forward to during the first few weeks.
- Put a note in your diary to ring the young person regularly after the initial move and offer to meet up with them.
- Schedule some future meetings in the diary so the young person knows you aren't abandoning them, and make it clear that you will still be around to offer support.

TIP 10

Provide ongoing support and help young people create strategies for living by themselves

For years, A National Voice has been expressing serious concerns about the lack of a safety net for young people once they leave care. So many young

> *people end up losing their tenancy because they fall*
> *into rent arrears or sometimes, because they just*
> *don't have enough support and guidance, their*
> *friends (and I use that word loosely) take over the*
> *property, creating noise nuisance or other issues.*
> *Then, of course, their local authority, who, let us not*
> *forget, is their corporate parent, evicts them.*
>
> *Benni-Jo Tyler, Young Person's Involvement Worker for Shaftesbury*
> *Young People.*

See the step into independent living as a start not an end

How many parents close the door when their child sets off for college or moves into their first flat and says, 'Well that's my job done. I hope they get on OK.' The average parent will be popping round or picking up the phone saying, 'Have you got enough to eat? What's the place like, and have you met the neighbours yet? You forgot to pack your pyjamas – do you want me to bring them round to you?'

Young people leaving care often have no one to say and do these things. It is therefore crucial to continue to offer support after they move into their own accommodation. The move is not an end to the process but the beginning of a new stage in your work with them.

- Make sure young people are truly ready to leave their placement and don't feel forced out. This has been said in previous chapters but it can't be repeated often enough.
- Stay in regular contact during the early stages after a young person moves into their new accommodation – be it a flat, bedsit, shared house or university campus.
- Continue to show an interest in the young person's course, job or search for employment and check that they are receiving support from appropriate agencies. Ask about the latter in some detail, as the young person may not be getting the help they need but don't realise that the level of intervention is insufficient.
- If it is appropriate to decrease the amount of contact gradually over a planned period of time, schedule in future meetings so the

young person knows you will be staying in touch.

> *Aftercare team should continue past 21, until 24 to 25 for everyone, including young parents, not just those at uni.*
>
> *Young person, from 'What makes the difference, Care Matters Green Paper Young People's Consultation Events Feedback Report'*

- Don't assume that because a young person seemed independent and capable before they started living alone that they will cope well with the transition to adult life. Isolation and the pressures of trying to make ends meet can quickly undercut their confidence and leave them feeling overwhelmed.
- Try to create a relationship where the young person feels able to tell you when things are going wrong. If they feel you have a particular picture of them, e.g. 'X is always so capable and reliable', then they will find it difficult to let you know when things are not so rosy. Demonstrate clearly that you have faith in young people and you recognise their skills, but make it clear that everyone is entitled to be human and that it's fine – and mature – to ask for help.
- Keep the young person feeling involved by informing them of forthcoming activities, training opportunities, etc. You could produce a type of "round-robin" letter each month for care leavers who are living independently, with updates about events and activities and maybe any relevant benefit or legislation news that might interest them. Make it as easy for yourself as possible by having a set of labels photocopied and having a pro forma for the newsletter set up on your computer. Every time you hear about an event or opportunity, type in a couple of lines about it – and keep it simple. The less work you create for yourself, the more likely you are to manage to send it out.
- Are there ways you could help care leavers network so they could support one another? Could you hold a few events for recent care leavers and those preparing for the move to meet each other and hopefully develop friendships? Also think about inviting young

people to support or befriend each other. As described in the chapter on Tip 5, there are schemes for more experienced care leavers to mentor those in the earlier stages of the process, but, as pointed out by researchers, mentoring doesn't always need to be a formal relationship in order to be beneficial.

> *She'd always seemed such a capable young person. I was amazed how much she struggled at the beginning with the course – I think it was just too much, the new environment, the responsibilities of managing her own finances, it just all got too much for her... you realise then how young and how vulnerable these young people really are.*
>
> Leaving Care Worker

Help young people avoid isolation

Isolation is one of the biggest issues affecting young people who begin to live independently for the first time. The excitement of having their own place and preparing for the move may very soon dissolve into a sense of loneliness and isolation if you haven't helped them prepare for this. This loneliness can make young people vulnerable in a number of ways. They may be prone to depression or may start to rely on alcohol or drugs to help them cope. They may stop caring about the need to manage their budget and start running up debts. The need to be with other people may also make them susceptible to people who may see their new home as somewhere to party, deal drugs or just make a general nuisance of themselves. It will then be the young person with the tenancy who faces complaints from neighbours, mounting bills and threats of eviction – long after these "friends" have moved on to other vulnerable people. Even if it is actually their "real" friends who are visiting, a young person feeling isolated is more likely to agree to having a large party or playing music loudly if they feel this will encourage their friends to visit more often.

By staying in regular contact and having discussions with care leavers about how things are working out, you keep the door open for them to talk to you about any concerns they have. However, some of these issues may not be presented as problems and the young person who tells you what a fantastic time they are having with friends round all the time may equally be showing warning signs. Try not to lecture, but give the young person opportunities to think about what they really want and need in this situation, and to think through possible consequences of what is happening. Don't expect them to thank you for pointing out that things are going wrong. They may not be able to admit that they are making a mistake, but later on they will probably think about and start to make small changes.

> *After growing up moving from family to family, school to school and social worker to social worker, the most exciting thing for me was the thought of getting my own tenancy – having my own place for the first time. And if it wasn't for the support from the nice people around me and many second chances, I would not have managed with the money and the forms and the cooking type of stuff. It's taken me nearly four years of living alone to get things right. But I notice that my mate's family still give him loads of emotional and financial support – even though he's 22 like me.*
>
> Young person, taken from 'There's no place like Home', published by A National Voice

Preventing isolation: contact with friends and family

In previous chapters, ideas have been given for helping young people to prepare for the move – such as having a friend stay overnight on their first night. It is worth helping them to regard their social life as an area of their life they need to manage in the same way as they manage household tasks, attending training or studying. Encourage them to allocate sufficient time for themselves and planning ahead to spend time with friends.

Another key issue around moving out of public care is around the links young people have with their family. Hopefully, good work has already been done to ensure that the young person you start working with has contact with the important people in their lives – but never assume this. Research shows that many young people are not getting the amount or type of contact they would like.

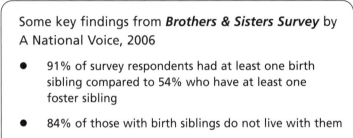

Some key findings from *Brothers & Sisters Survey* by A National Voice, 2006

- 91% of survey respondents had at least one birth sibling compared to 54% who have at least one foster sibling

- 84% of those with birth siblings do not live with them

- 62% of those with foster siblings do not live withthem

- 83% of respondents who do not live with their birth siblings would like to see more of them

- 38% of respondents who do not live with their foster siblings would like to see more of them

Some young people who have never had their own home may not think about inviting friends over for a simple meal. So don't forget to suggest this – along with ideas about sharing out the menu so that different people cook a course each.

Renewing contact with friends or family after a break can be a sensitive and complex issue. As a worker, you will know that young people will need support to manage expectations and deal with possible rejection or disappointment.

> *She was that chuffed when her big sister got in touch and she was wanting to be over there every weekend, and had all these big plans about moving back there. Then her sister had a baby and things changed. She didn't want my little lass there so often, and gradually the contact stopped.*
>
> Foster carer

Ensure that young people receive appropriate support if they are attempting to contact relatives they haven't seen for a while. Local authority aftercare services or specialist services from organisations like Barnardo's, NCH, the Post Adoption Centre, etc may be able to offer support.

Encourage young people to be flexible about their options. They may strongly wish to live close to their birth family, but have they fully considered the implications? What if the family moves or they fall out with them? Would siblings expect to move in with them? Would it be better to be somewhere close but not too close?

Returning to a home area may also bring young people back into contact with former friends or people who have not had a positive influence on their lives. These issues need to be weighed up carefully.

The importance of friendships is sometimes overlooked when we think about contact issues for care leavers. However, the relationship with a school friend or relationships developed with other young people in their residential home or foster family can be very supportive and nurturing. Sometimes it will be extremely valuable to help a young person to track down a good friend they have lost touch with or to find accommodation close to their best friend.

People with learning disabilities often lose many important relationships during the transition from children's to adult services. Unless someone takes the time to find out who matters to them, you will not be able to help them maintain relationships with those people.

Some young people are able to maintain close links with their foster carers or staff in residential homes. These relationships may have their ups and downs in the way all relationships do, so be aware of the importance of asking about a young person's important relationships and offering the opportunity to talk through any problems.

Sadly, some young people may be involved in court cases with relatives or former carers after they move into young adult lives. These can be very painful times for them, so try to ensure they have appropriate sources of support.

For young people who have no family or close friends to rely on, a befriending scheme or mentoring from an older care leaver may be beneficial during this time.

The Care Leavers Association runs a website to enable people who have left care to get in touch with friends from their childhood (www.careleaversreunited.com).

Who do young people call when they have a problem?

Who do young people call if they have a problem? If you can't answer this question, then you may need to identify appropriate sources of support. And if you find yourself telling young people that they are always welcome to call you – but gritting your teeth as you do so because you already feel overwhelmed – then this isn't going to be the best situation in the long run. However, it is an issue that needs to be faced, and if you find yourself struggling with it alone, then you need to discuss it with your supervisor and other team members.

If you really cannot continue offering support to care leavers as they grow older, at least make sure that you have put them in touch with organisations that can provide this support and create networking opportunities – such as A National Voice, Voices from Care Cymru, Who Cares? Scotland, etc. – depending on where the young person lives.

When young people have their own children

They're my corporate parents, they brought me up,

> *but now they say I don't have the skills to look after my own child. So what sort of parent have they been?*
>
> *Care-experienced young woman*

A disproportionately high level of care leavers have their own children at an early age. There are many reasons for this, but what is clear is that many young people feel abandoned by their corporate parent when they become young parents.

Don't assume that care-experienced young people will be unfit parents. Their own negative experiences may make them determined to provide excellent parenting to their own children.

Don't greet the news that a young woman is pregnant as a disaster. Young people aren't stupid and they know what struggles they are likely to face as young parents. This is a time when they need support rather than lectures about how difficult this is going to be.

Some young people may not be suited to parenthood but others will make a success of it. In order to succeed they need encouragement, not threats and messages of gloom and doom.

Find out how the young woman feels about the pregnancy before you offer advice on abortion or adoption services or start listing the problems she will face. Some young women will have decided they want to keep their child and won't be receptive to other options if they are presented too soon or too forcefully. You may feel this is the wrong time and the wrong situation for a young woman to have a child, but she may have very strong moral, religious or even humanistic views about the rights of the unborn child – or just a sense that it would be inappropriate to abort her baby. Try to respect this and recognise if you or others are pressurising her to make decisions that go against her feelings.

Don't be too hasty to involve child protection services or put the unborn baby of a care-experienced young woman on the child protection register. You may find yourself in a difficult position because of your authority or agency's child protection procedures, but you also need to remember that the young woman involved is now an adult and deserves to be treated in this way.

If a young woman plans to keep her baby, she needs support to help her be the best parent possible (even if you personally don't feel this is the best course of action). There are projects that provide information and advice for young parents, for example, the Young Parents Network run by Barnardo's in Belfast (www.barnardos.org.uk/young parentsbelfast).

A young woman who faces a battle about keeping her child may benefit considerably from early support from an advocate. Be prepared to put her in touch with either your local advocacy service or a national service. Even if you have doubts about her suitability to parent, she still deserves the right to make the very best case possible to keep her child, and to receive appropriate support to do this.

If a young woman decides to have an abortion or place a child for adoption, make sure that she receives plenty of support around this time. For someone who has faced rejection and feelings of being unwanted, this may stir up a raft of painful emotions.

Even if you support a young woman's decision to place her baby for adoption or fostering, it is still important to recognise the pain this will cause her. It might be hard explaining this to her, as she may expect you to take her side. But be clear that you will still support her emotionally or you'll find other people who can do so.

Your knowledge of a young woman's strengths and coping abilities may be useful evidence in helping other professionals to make decisions. Be prepared to offer this information as other professionals may not be aware of your relationship with her.

Even if you don't agree with a young woman's decision to keep her child, make sure you are not being obstructive. Be prepared to help her access benefits and grants and accompany her to initial meetings about claiming them.

Never forget that the children of your corporate children are your corporate grandchildren. Most families welcome a grandchild into the family even if they have some personal worries about how the young parent may cope. Simple things like accompanying them to buy baby clothes or a pram can mean a great deal to them and help them recognise that you are still there to support them.

> *I'll leave aside the various debates about what can be done to reduce the numbers of care-experienced young people becoming parents and why looked after young people become parents earlier than other young people. The Fostering Network has an excellent report covering these issues... What I would like to say, however, is that when my children make me a grandparent I won't tell them their life is over, and that all they can expect from their lives now are dirty nappies and benefits. I won't refuse to help them buy a pram on the grounds that they need to claim Income Support now that they have a baby, and I won't subject them to gruelling child protection procedures, question their suitability as parents and fast track them through to the Child Protection Register or adoption services.*
>
> *I will support them, care for them and their child, talk to them about parenting classes and support groups. The minute my children become parents, I become a grandparent. The minute your corporate children become parents, you become corporate grandparents! Please do for these children what you would do for your own grandchildren!*
>
> *Benni-Jo Tyler, Young Person's Involvement Worker for Shaftesbury Young People*

Be optimistic abut young people's future

People have a tendency to fulfil the roles others create for them. So if a young person moves into adult life with the impression that you think they're destined to fail or will never make anything of themselves, it is more likely they will fulfil the prophecy. Sadly, it is only a very few – mainly characters in books and films – who take the "I'll show them" approach of proving everyone wrong. And this isn't a chance you want to take with a young person's life.

Believe in, and expect the best for, every young person you work with, but allow them space to learn from their mistakes. Above all, make sure they realise you appreciate and like them for who they are (even if you don't always like what they do) – because that level of unconditional acceptance is probably the greatest gift we can give anyone.

Essential guides for care leavers

Getting Sorted! and Getting More Sorted!
Rebecca Davidson
Illustrated by Fran Orford

For children and young people who have not benefited from stable and continuous family support, these books are the ultimate "portable parent". They are packed with practical advice and information, easy to read and use, and illustrated with highly original cartoons.

Getting Sorted! is aimed at young people who are either moving into foster or residential care or are moving out to live on their own for the first time. It covers a wide range of practical day-to-day issues such as: washing clothes; cleaning and tidying; diet and food preparation; managing money; getting online; and what to do in an emergency.

Getting More Sorted! is aimed at older teenagers and covers the practical concerns of moving on in life, such as: finding accommodation; relationships and sexual health; applying for a place at college or university; and getting a job.

Both books also address important broader issues such as staying safe, keeping healthy and building self-esteem.

£9.95 EACH   144 PAGES 198 X 129MM
ISBN 1 903699 95 9/1 905664 11 7

BUY BOTH FOR £15!

Order at www.baaf.org.uk or phone Publications on 020 7421 2604 or email pubs.sales@baaf.org.uk.

Useful organisations

GENERAL HELP AND ADVICE

Albert Kennedy Trust

Runs schemes to find foster carers, lodgings and housing for lesbian, gay and bisexual young people.
Unit 305a Hatton Square
16/16a Baldwin Gardens
London EC1N 7RJ
Tel: 020 7831 6562
www.akt.org.uk

Care for Life

A Christian charity which provides a number of social caring and educational projects for young people.
53 Romney Street
London SW1P 3RF
Tel: 020 7233 0455
www.care.org.uk

Childline

A free and confidential 24-hour helpline for children and young people.
Freephone: 0800 1111
www.childline.org.uk

Children's Legal Centre

Provides legal advice and information to children, young people and their carers.
University of Essex
Wivenhoe Park
Colchester CO4 3SQ
Freephone: 0800 783 2187
www.childrenslegalcentre.com

Citizens Advice Bureaux

Provides free, independent information and advice on legal, money and other problems.
Find your local CAB
www.citizensadvice.org.uk

Connexions

Offers advice on education, careers, housing, money and health for 13–19-year-olds.
Freephone: 0808 001 3219
www.connexions.gov.uk

Lesbian and Gay Switchboard

A 24-hour helpline offering support, advice and information to lesbians, gay men and bisexuals.
Tel: 020 7837 7324
www.llgs.org.uk

MIND

Works to advance the views and needs of people with mental health problems, and provides advice and support.
15–19 Broadway
London E15 4BQ
Tel: 0845 766 0163
9.15am–5.15pm Mon–Fri
www.mind.org.uk

National Debt Line

Provides free, confidential and independent advice on dealing with debt problems.
Freephone: 0808 080 4000
www.nationaldebtline.co.uk

Rape Crisis Centre

Look in Yellow Pages under 'R' for your local branch.

Refuge

Provides a 24-hour domestic violence helpline for women and children, and a network of safe houses.
Freephone: 0808 200 0247
www.refuge.org.uk

Refugee Council

Offers help and support to asylum seekers and refugees.
240–250 Ferndale Road
London SW9 8BB
Tel: 020 7346 6700
www.refugeecouncil.org.uk

Shelter

Provides a 24-hour national housing service.
Freephone: 0808 800 4444
www.shelter.org.uk

Women's Aid

Works to end domestic violence against women and children, and provides help and advice.
Freephone: 0808 200 0247
www.womensaid.org.uk

FOR YOUNG PEOPLE IN CARE / LEAVING CARE

CareLaw.org.uk
A website that provides
information on rights and legal
matters for young people in care
or leaving care.
www.carelaw.co.uk

Care Leavers Association
Offers support, information, help
with accessing childhood case
records, and aims to raise public
awareness of care leavers needs.
Care Leavers Association
Suite F113
23 New Mount Street
Manchester M4 4DE
Tel: 0161 953 4047
www.careleavers.com

Care Leavers Reunited
A website run by the care leavers
association to help those who
have been in care to make
contact with past friends.
www.careleaversreunited.com

**The Fostering Network Young
People's Project
(England and Wales)**
Works with young people on a
number of projects aimed at
allowing young people's voices to
be heard.
87 Blackfriars Road
London SE1 8HA
Tel: 020 7620 6400
www.fostering.net/activities/engl
and/youngpeople.php

**The Fostering Network's
Young People's Project
(Scotland)**
Second Floor
Ingram House
227 Ingram Street
Glasgow G1 1DA
Tel: 0141 204 1400
www.fostering.net/activities/scotl
and/young_people/

LeavingHome.info
An online guide to leaving care
and housing for young people in
Scotland, run by the Scottish
Council for Single Homeless.
www.leavinghome.info

A National Voice

Campaigns for the rights of care leavers, and offers advice and information.
Central Hall
Oldham Street
Manchester M1 1JQ
Tel: 0161 237 5577
www.anationalvoice.org

The Scottish Throughcare and Aftercare Forum

Aims to improve support for young people leaving care in Scotland .
37 Otago Street
Glasgow G12 8JJ
Tel: 0141 357 4124
www.scottishthroughcare.org.uk/youth.php

Voice (formerly Voice for the Child in Care)

Works with children and young people in care to support them and promote their views.
Unit 4, Pride Court
80–82 White Lion Street
London N1 9PF
Freephone: 0808 800 5792
www.voiceyp.org.uk

The Who Cares? Trust

Aims to improve the lives of children and young people in residential and foster care. Kemp House
152–160 City Road
London EC1V 2NP
Tel: 020 7251 3117
www.thewhocarestrust.org.uk

Useful resources for young people on sexual health and pregnancy, education and employment and volunteering, drugs and alcohol, and much more are available in *Getting Sorted!* and *Getting More Sorted!* (see p. 110).